Blood, Bone And Bewitchment

By

Delfino Mark
Anthony Drakkar

ISBN

Hardcover: 978-1-967616-62-6
Paperback: 978-1-967616-61-9

DEDICATION

"For my daughter, Saphiera-may you always see the magic in
life. Never lose that spark of the divine that shines in your
eyes. I love you, always and forever."

ACKNOWLEDGMENT

I would like to acknowledge the authors Freya Aswynn and Bernard King for their writings and knowledge of the Elder Furhark. Through them, I was truly able to find my own path to the ancient mysteries. May the old God's light your path to the next life and beyond.

Contents

PREFACE

Here in these pages is my own personal "Galdrabok" or "Book of Shadows." Over the span of many years, I've compiled a number of Rites and spells I feel every witch or wizard should read. This is not the end-all-be-all of the witchcraft world, but I'm confident you'll get out of this book what it is you want. Everything I was first looking for in the craft is here fused together in a sort of "eclectic" way.

Most books you buy are all the same. You get a lot of history about the person's path, some pages on how they do rituals for the sabbats, and a couple of spells. Usually, the spells are love, luck, money, healing, etc.

In this book, you'll find everything you need to do Asatruar- spellcraft, including herbs, incense, oils, runes, pictures of tarot cards, Gods, chants, invocations, and materials to do so. I've touched on the sacred "Laws of Old" and given a description of how to build or make anything you might need that's out of the ordinary. Consider this "A Modern Norseman's Spell Book".

I only scraped the surface of the runes because there have been many books written on the subject already. The same goes for all the history and myths. To continue to do so just to fill some pages doesn't appeal to me in the slightest. Freya Aswynn, Ed Thorsson, Bernard King, and Paul Rhys Mountfort are a few of the best in the business. I'll leave it to the professionals. I have included enough of these things to get you by and into casting and ritual.

I've thrown in personal drawings of the tarot cards for quick reference, as well as to photocopy if needed. No one wants to buy a whole deck just for one or two cards. I'm confident that you'll almost never come across another

Asatruar-based spell book quite like this in your lifetime. As a bonus, I've included the rune spells straight out of the Havamal that pertain to each of my own. Each of these is a rune spell on its own.

I did not include a page at the beginning of each spell or rite telling you what you need for one reason...I want you to read through them completely. You must first understand what it is you're doing before you do it. I do not believe in doing any type of Spellcraft halfway. Read each section in its entirety before diving in head-first.

Pleases enjoy, and remember...always be careful when working with the craft...that which goes out always comes back!

CHAPTER 1:

THE LAWS OF OLD

These are the laws handed down from generation to generation. The 26 laws of how to live honourably. As well as nine noble virtues and six goals of life one should strive for. In fact, the NNV and the 6 Goals were taught to me verbally.

The Norse believed in being good to each other and looking after one's family and folk. Women and men were equal in day-to-day life. In fact, even their names, Weavemen and Weapmen, are similar.

REDE OF HONOUR

In all that you do, consider its benefit or harm upon yourself, your children, and your people.

All that which you do will return to you, sooner or later, for good or for ill. So, strive always to do good to others, or at least strive always to be just.

Be honest with yourself and with others. "This above all; to thine own self be true!"

Humankind, and especially your own family and folk, has the spark of divinity within it. Protect and nurture that spark.

Give your word sparingly, and adhere to it like iron.

In the world, your first trust and responsibility should be to your own people. Yet, be kind and proper to others whenever possible.

What you have, hold!

Pass on to others only those words which you have personally verified.

Be honest with others, and let them know that you expect honesty in return, always.

The fury of the moment plays folly with the truth; to keep one's head is a virtue.

Know which battles should be fought and which battles should be avoided. Also, know when to break off a conflict. There are times when the minions of chaos are simply too strong or when fate is absolutely unavoidable.

When you gain power, use it carefully and use it well.

Courage and honour endure forever. Their echoes remain when the mountains have crumbled to dust.

Pledge friendship and your services to those who are worthy. Strengthen others of your people, and they will strengthen you.

Love and care for your family always, and have the fierceness of a wolf in their protection.

Honour yourself, have pride in yourself, do your best, and forgive yourself when you must.

Try always to be above reproach in the eyes of the world.

Those of our people should always endeavour to settle any differences among themselves quietly and peaceably.

The laws of the land should be obeyed whenever possible and reason, for in the main, they have been chosen with wisdom.

Have pride in yourself, your family, and your folk. They are your promise for the future.

Do not neglect your mate and children.

Every one of our people should work according to the best that s/he can do, no matter how small or how great. We are all in this world together, so we must always help each other along.

One advances individually and collectively only by living in harmony with the natural order of the world.

The seeking of wisdom is a high virtue. Love of truth, honour, courage, and loyalty are the hallmarks of the noble soul.

Be prepared for whatever the future brings.

Life, with all its joys, struggles, and ambiguities, is to be embraced and lived to the fullest!

THE NINE NOBLE VIRTUES

TRUTH

~

COURAGE

HONOUR

~

FEDALITY

GENEROUSITY

~

INDUSTRIOUSNESS

~

DISCIPLINE

SELF RELIANCE

~

PERSEVERANCE

THE 6 FOLD GOLDS

The Right: the right to follow the true and just laws for the benefit of all.

Wisdom: the right to further our knowledge

Might: not just "Might is Right," the right to work our strengths to benefit ourselves and people.

Harvest: the right harvest our rewards. "All that we do come back to us!"

Firth: the harmony and well-being that comes from living "good." The peace and prosperity that comes from living a true and noble life.

Love: Love of life. Embracing the essence of life. Always be enthusiastic about life, for good or ill. Life is to be experienced.

CHAPTER 2:

CASTING YOUR CIRCLE

In this chapter, you'll learn how to call the Fairies into your space, call Odin the Grey Wanderer, and call the Quarters. You'll also be taught an "Invoking of the Quarters" for those special rites and important spells. I also threw in a basic altar setup and ritual area I like to use for most of my rites and spells.

THE RITUAL AREA

I like to use torches with banners on them for the Runes I'm using

MY BASIC ALTAR

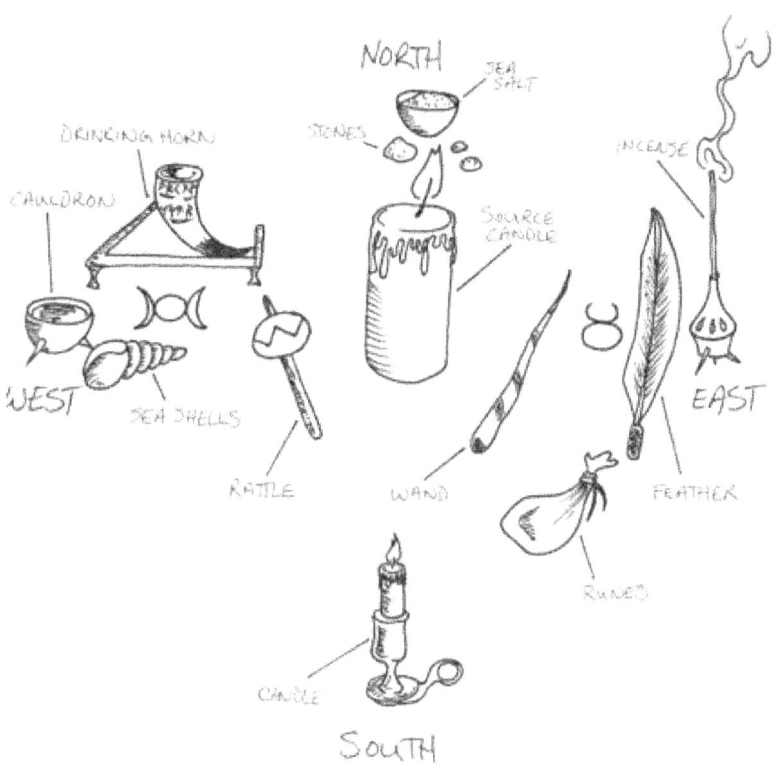

NORTH

SEA SALT

STONES

DRINKING HORN

CAULDRON

SOURCE CANDLE

INCENSE

WEST

SEA SHELLS

RATTLE

WAND

FEATHER

EAST

RUNES

CANDLE

SOUTH

FAIRY SUMMONS

"Come, little fairies be with me here,

Come, little fairies, there's nothing to fear.

Milk and honey are gifts

I'll bring,

Help me make my magik sing.

Spells and rites are my desire,

Take my power higher and higher.

Make it strong and make it fast,

Make it swift and make it last.

Take it high and take it low,

Do this task but not too slow.

Help my quest by day and night,

Wrapped in the warmth of moonlight.

Speak to the gods and carry my tunes,

Incantations and bloody runes.

Come little fairies, come to me; hear my call, so mote it be!"

Offerings:

Milk-honey-silver (anything shiny)

NEVER: use broom herb!!!

CALLING OF THE GREY WANDERER

"O far traveling, sky-cloaked wanderer

From the far, ancient lands,

We call you across mountain and forest;

And the far, limitless grasslands;

We call you across distant times,

And a hundred, hundred, slow turnings

Of the vast spindle of the sky.

We call to you in the lands of mystery

Where ravens wheel in darkling skies,

And the far calling of wolves,

Echoing eldritch through crisp night wind,

Brings close the strange far worlds

Where humankind never has trod.

We call to you beyond the distant icy tundra And the vast plains of snow.

Beneath the unearthly rippling and flowing Of the dark northern skies' boreal lights,

To the golden gates of far Valhall Where the shimmering bridge of rainbow Links the dark middle earth of men

With the shining realms of the gods. Come to me now and be with me here, Great Odin!"

CALLING QUARTERS

*To draw runes in the air, face the quarter, and use numbers to draw properly.

*Please remember that I follow Asatru, and we tend to start in the East.

*As you say the welcome, draw the solar cross at each of the four quarters.

AIR:

Rune- GEBO

"Welcome spirits of Air, welcome Odin, guardian of the East. As I am of thought and breath, we are kith and kin. I call upon you to watch over me, aid, and protect me in my work!" "I call you spirits of Air, guardians of wind. Hail Odin! Hail Odin! "

FIRE:

Rune- Sowulo

"Welcome spirits of Fire, welcome Dvalin, guardian of the South. As I am of warmth and energy, we are kith and kin. I call upon you to watch over me, aid, and protect me in my work!

"I call you spirits of Fire, guardians of flame.

Hail Dvalin! Hail Odin!"

WATER:

Rune-Laguz

"Welcome spirits of Water, welcome Dain, guardian of the West. As I am of water and blood, we are kith and kin. I call upon you to watch over me, aid, and protect me in my work!" "I call you, spirits of Water, guardians of the sea.

Hail Dain! Hail Odin!"

EARTH:

Rune-Isa

"Welcome spirits of Earth, welcome Asvind, guardian of the North. As I am of flesh and bone, we are kith and kin. I call upon you to watch over me, aid, and protect me in my work!" "I call you spirits of Earth, guardians of stone.

With Hail Asvind! Hail Odin!"

I also raise the energy from Gaia to the Sky Father's hands, starting on the ground and rising slowly...

"MMMMMMAAAAAAAHHHHHHH!"

Then from Father Sky to Gaia using hands opposite... "AAAAAAAAHHHHHMMMMM!"

This is when I use the symbol of Spirit and say... "AAAAAAWWWWWEEEENNNN!"

To undo the quarters, just say...

"Thank you, spirits of _____, for being here and aiding in my magikal work. As you depart to your lovely realms, harming no one on your way, may you find peace, love, and harmony. So, mote it be!"

Havamal-stanzas-142

"The runes you must find and the meaningful letter,

a very great letter, a very powerful letter, which the mighty sage stained and the powerful gods made, and the runemaster of the gods carved out

Havamal-stanzas-143

Odin for the Aesir,

and Dain for the elves,

Dvalin for the Dwarves,

Asvind for the giants,

I myself carved some.

INVOKING THE POWER OF THE 4 QUARTERS

"Odin, grant me your wisdom and intelligence. Patron of those who write and sing, rune-master, whose craft was learned by self-sacrifice and dedication; show me the words of power. Lead me on the path of creativity. Stand by me at initiation into realms of magik. Let me call upon your wisdom and magik. All-seeing, Great Father, hear my call!"

"Dvalin, grant me your will and passion. Hammers ring in caverns deep, where you, dwarves, your watch to keep. Teach me magik of earth and stone, gems and metals, Earth- Mothers bone. From deep mountain caves of yore. A friend I'll be, and secrets keep if you teach me magik deep. Dwarves of knowledge strong and bold, come as once you did of old!"

"Dain, grant me your power over emotions and persuasion. Light elves, from dark forests shady, come to me, both Lord and Lady. Dressed in magik clothes and flowers, teach me in the twilight hours. Sing to me an Eldritch tune as the clouds flow past the moon. Whisper magik of the land, mushroom ring, and wooded strand. Light elves, from the forest shady, come to me, both Lord and Lady!"

"Asvind, grant me your strength and solidness of stone. Giants of the mountain pass, give me strength and make it last. Solid as the largest stone, help me claim my earthy throne. Let no man stand before my dreams; let knowledge of ages flow like streams. Giants of the mountain pass, give strength, and make it last!"

*As far as I'm concerned, all of these depictions are Odin in his many forms for all races. Though, some believe because "Asvind" means friend that, it represents Mimir, the giant. I feel that as "All-Father," Odin would have a different name and form for all who pray to him.

"Dain, grant me your power over emotions and persuasion. Light elves, from dark forests shady, come to me, both Lord and Lady. Dressed in magik clothes and flowers, teach me in the twilight hours. Sing to me an Eldritch tune as the clouds flow past the moon. Whisper magik of the land, mushroom ring, and wooded strand. Light elves, from the forest shady, come to me, both Lord and Lady!"

"Asvind, grant me your strength and solidness of stone. Giants of the mountain pass, give me strength and make it last. Solid as the largest stone, help me claim my earthy throne. Let no man stand before my dreams; let knowledge of ages flow like streams. Giants of the mountain pass, give strength, and make it last!"

*As far as I'm concerned, all of these depictions are Odin in his many forms for all races. Though, some believe because "Asvind" means friend that, it represents Mimir, the giant. I feel that as "All-Father," Odin would have a different name and form for all who pray to him.

CHAPTER 3:

SPELLCRAFT BASICS

Here I touch on the basics of spellcraft just to get you started as it pertains to this book overall. A couple of lessons that I feel are important in the big scheme of things. I've also added some poems for your reading pleasure.

Over the years, I've picked up some ideas from other paths and different Godis and Godias, making this book quite eclectic in nature.

CHARGE OF THE GODDESS

Listen to the words of the great mother; She who was of old called Artemis, Astarte, Athene, Dione, Melusine, Aphrodite, Cerridwen, Dana, Arionrod, Isis, Brede, and by many other names:

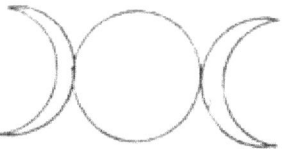

Whenever you have need of anything, once in the month, and better it is when the moon is full, then shall you assemble in some secret place and adore the spirit of me who am Queen of all witches. There shall you assemble, you who feign to learn all sorcery yet have not won its deepest secrets; to these, I will teach things that are yet unknown. And you shall be free from slavery; and as a sign that you be really free, you shall be naked in your rites. You shall dance, sing, feast, make music, and love in my praise. For mine is the ecstasy of the spirit, and mine also is joy on earth-for my law is love unto all beings. Keep pure your highest ideal, strive ever towards it- let naught stop you or turn you aside. For mine is the secret door which opens on the land of youth, and mine is the cup of the wine of life, the cauldron of Cerridwen, which is the holy grail of immortality. I am the gracious goddess who gives the gift of joy unto the hearts of my children. Upon earth, I give the knowledge of the spirit eternal. Beyond death, I give peace and freedom and reunion with those who have gone before. Nor do I demand sacrifice, for behold: I am the mother of all living, my love is poured out upon the earth.

Hear you the words of the star goddess; she in the dust of whose feet are the hosts of heaven and shoe body encircles the universe:

I, who am the beauty of the green earth and the white moon among the stars and the mystery of the waters and the desire of the heart of creation, call unto your soul: arise and come unto me, for I am the soul of nature who gives life to the universe. From me, all things proceed, and unto me, all things must return.

Before my face, beloved of the gods and my children, let your innermost divine self be enfolded in the rapture of the infinite. Let my worship be in the heart that rejoices, for behold, all acts of love and pleasure are my rituals. And therefore, let thereby beauty and strength, power and compassion, honor and humility, mirth and reverence within you. And you who think to seek for me, know your seeking and yearning will not avail you unless you know the mystery: that if that which you seek you find not within you, then you will never find it without you. For behold, I have been with you since the beginning and I am that which attained at the end of desire.

THE NINE WORLDS

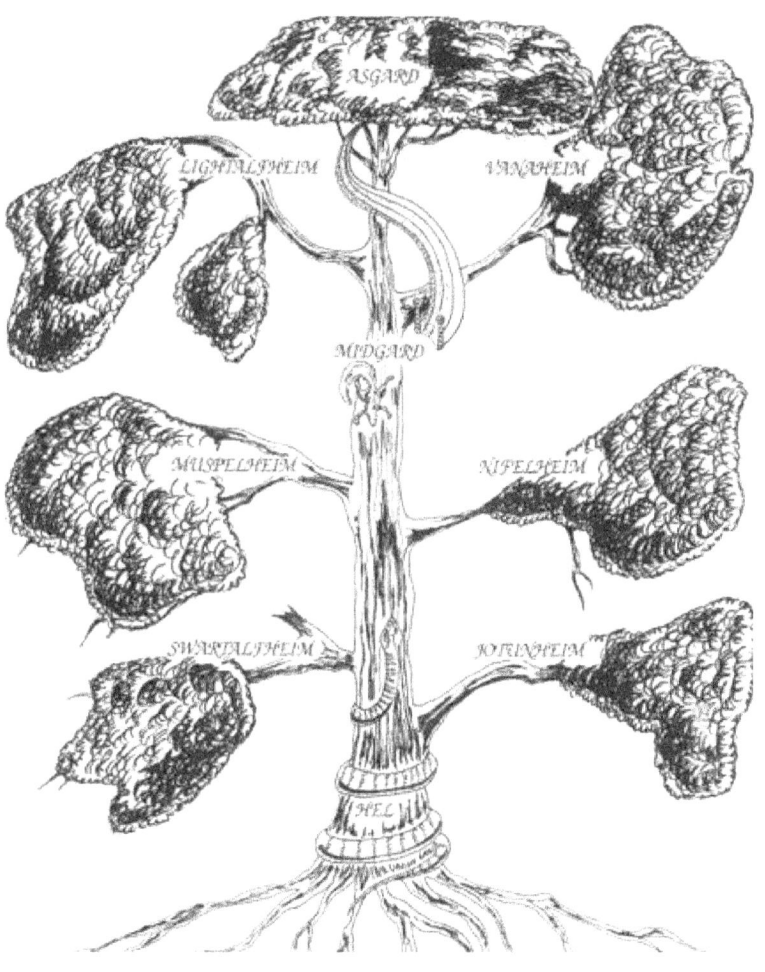

WITCHES' PYRAMID

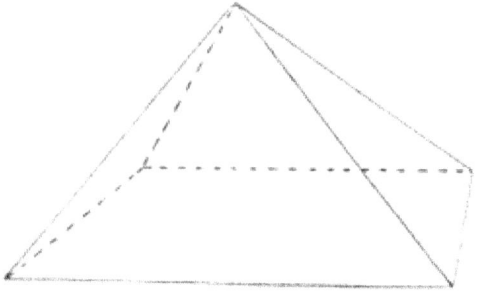

*Also called the powers (or virtues) of the magus (or sphinx)

To know, to will, to dare, to keep silent (imagination, will, faith, silence)

Base- Desire (dark or spirit)

Face 1- Knowledge, imagination (D/B & Air)

Face 2- Will; discipline (D/B & Fire)

Face 3- Faith, Daring (D/B & Water)

Face 4- Silence, listening (D/B & Earth)

Apex- Attainment (Bright or spirit)

*These are things that must be taken into consideration when doing any type of spellcraft. The number one to me is silence. Never tell anyone outside of the circle what you're doing. If things go wrong, you will be blamed.

WITCHES' WHEEL

The Witches' sigil is easy to use, and you can create your own types of runes and symbols.

I.e. Health-   Joy-A

Just start with the first letter, and then draw a line connecting the continuing letters in order. The line starts with a and ends with

BLACK MIRROR

*This is to create your own Black Mirror for scrying and talking to spirits.

1. Take a piece of mirror.

2. Scratch off the silver backing

3. Wash it with sea salt water

4. Leave it to dry in the light of a full moon

5. Paint the back with black paint mixed with a drop of your

6. Cover the back with black felt and fit it into the frame."

*There you go, you're done. I like using a mirror instead of just regular glass because it was made to reflect. Always keep the mirror covered with black cloth when you're not using it.

*Never let the sunlight touch your mirror. This will destroy it!!! *The B is a must to tune the mirror to you!

VANA-GODDESS

She's my light in the darkness. Like the spirits of my ancestors, She watches over me.

She's my armour in battle. Like the Shield Maidens she commands, She protects me always.

She's my passion in this life. Like the fires in the depths of Earth, She shows me great rapture.

She's my first mature true love. Like the four Dwarves of Brisingamen, She seduces me with ease.

She's my companion, confidant. Like her two cats, Amber and Honey, She always stands by me.

ETERNALLY

I am here, my Goddess, Waiting for you,

Searching for you,

Yearning for you.

I wish to be in your arms,

Close to you,

Touching you, Embracing you.

I can smell your breath On my face,

On my hands, On my loins.

I can taste you, Sweet on my lips, As we move together,
Towards rapture.

I give myself to you. Every part of me, Mind, body, and spirit,
I am yours eternally.

CHAPTER 4:

THE VIKING ORACLE

In this section, I only scratch the surface of the runes and the meanings of them. There are a number of books out there on runes if that's what you're after. Many authors have years of knowledge. It's been done a hundred times, and I wasn't going to do it again just to fill some space in this book.

I've also included my own personal seals and other scripts used throughout history for your personal knowledge, as well as an explanation of how to carve your own runes. Don't be afraid to create your own runic system or alphabet. Magik is about experimenting with nature and energy.

CARVING YOUR OWN RUNES

*Here is a quick and easy way to carve your very own runes.

1. Take the wood of your choosing (it doesn't have to be Yew, but it would be nice)

2 Cut it into either circular or rectangle chips about % of an inch thick, an inch tall, and 4 of an inch wide.

3. Now, take your "V" type carving tool and begin with Fehu.

*Meditate on the meaning of the rune as you carve it. Put all your

energy into it. Maybe sing the names of each one as you go.

4. All the cuts on the runes are straight lines, so this should be easy. And always cut away from yourself...trust me.

5. Once they're carved, give it a quick sanding to smooth out the edges.

6. Take some "Red Okra" or just some regular non-toxic red paint or ink, add at least a drop of your BM to it, and mix it up. Now paint away.

*This will attune the runes to you and you only. Don't ever give them away. They'll never work properly for anyone else now.

*Women used to use their own menstrual blood to consecrate the runes in olden times.

*Havamal- stanza- 144

"Do you know how to carve? Do you know how to interpret,

Do you know how to stain? Do you know how to test out,

Do you know how to ask? Do you know how to sacrifice?

Do you know how to dispatch? Do you know how to slaughter?"

RUNES

*This will be a basic run-through of the Elder Futhark runes, some of their meanings, and uses.

Fehu: meaning- cattle, wealth

God/Goddess- Frey, Niord, Frejya

Fehu can be used in any spell or talisman involving wealth, business, job finding or promotion, achieving goals, etc. It could help to become more responsible. Used for disposable cash.

Phonetic value- F

Uruz: meaning-Aurochs

God/Goddess- Thor

Uruz is about strength. It could be used for sports or any physical activity. It can strengthen will or sexual virility. It can be used to strengthen a particular body part for healing or used in hunting.

Phonetic value-U

Thurisaz: meaning- a thorn, Giant

God/Goddess- Thor, Yimir

Thurisaz can be used in any endeavor that requires patience and discipline (study, addiction, meditation, dieting, etc.) It could be used to beat infections in general. Also used as the troll rune, of course.

Phonetic value-TH

Ansuz: meaning- a God (usually Odin)

Ansuz is used for success or wise decisions. Helps with mental illness and psychic endeavors.

Phonetic value-A

Raido: meaning- riding or journey God/Goddess- Odin

Raido is used for traveling; it can also help change one's life. It can help the passage of time or to the other side. It may also help with mental blocks and such.

Phonetic value-R

Kennaz: meaning- torch, light

God/Goddess- Hiemdal

Kennaz can help in creative endeavors. Casting light on a subject. It may help stimulate and circulate organs. Phonetic value-C, K

Gebo: meaning-gift

God/Goddess- Odin, Thor, Freyja

Gebo can be used in love spells, friendship spells, luck or gambling. Great for Binding two or more runes together. It may help heal bones, muscles, ligaments, and nerves.

Phonetic value-G

Wunjo: meaning- perfection, joy

God/Goddess- Odin, Freyja

Wunjo is great for spell work or talismans. It can be used to achieve any goal with other runes. It may help overall with any illness.

Phonetic value-V, W

Hagalaz: meaning- hail

God/Goddess- Hella, Urd (Norns)

Hagalaz is rarely used for positive because of its destructive nature. It could be used to destroy negative work, influence, energy, or patterns. You could surround it with positive runes to face any karma built up. Careful! Used in death rites and hexes. This is a very powerful rune.

Phonetic value-P

Nauthiz: meaning- need

God/Goddess- skuld (Norns)

Nauthiz usually represents that which you wish to be rid of, like Hagalaz. It could be used in a request to the Gods or Norns. Through necessity, things are created or invented.

Phonetic value-N

Isa: meaning- ice

God/Goddess- Verdandi (Norns)

Isa usually used to stop something, placed after runes for war, illness, ect. Only rune to negate Thurisaz; it can be used in self-defense or a pre-emptive strike.

Phonetic value-I

Jera: meaning- year, harvest

God/Goddess- Frey, Freyja (fertility)

Jera is used in change, moving along, and finding conclusions. Great for agriculture, work, and yearly events. When drawn forward, it can speed things up. When drawn backwards it will slow things down.

Phonetic value-J

Eihwaz: meaning- yew

God/Goddess- Odin, Uller

Eihwaz represents the tree of life, Yggdrasil. Used for initiation or to ease death. Great for psychic and magikal use.

Phonetic value-IE, Y

Pertho: meaning- secret, women, birth?

God/Goddess- Mimir, Norns

Pertho is used for women, possibly sexual or dysfunction. It may help memories of past life memories when used with Othila and Laguz. It can help greatly with divination and psychic abilities.

Phonetic value-P

Algiz: meaning- protection kinds.

God/Goddess-Valkyries

Algiz in magik is used for the protection or defense of all

Phonetic value-Z

Sowulo: meaning- sun, victory

God/Goddess-Thor, Sunna, Baldur

Strengthens any runes it's with. Used for success or victory in something. Great for healing. When doubled on top of itself, it represents the sun-wheel.

Phonetic value-S

Teiwaz: meaning- the God Tyr, justice

Teiwaz is used as a protection rune in battle. It can impart vitality and strength. It may help control pain. Also used in legal proceedings or anything for which you wish justice. Used in oaths.

Phonetic value-T

Berkana: meaning- Birch

God/Goddess-Berchta, Frigga

Berkana is a great healing rune, particularly for infections. It may help with conception and starting a new life. A talisman with three berkana runes invokes the power of the Goddess in all aspects.

Phonetic value-B

Ehwaz: meaning-horse, travel

God/Goddess- Sleipnir (Odin's horse)

Ehwaz holds great spiritual and astrological powers. Great for communication spells, or any spells for that matter. Good for a spiritual journey or astral travel. It can be used to send magik or strengthen and energize the circulatory system, including the heart.

Phonetic value-E

Mannaz: meaning- a man (Gen,)

God/Goddess- Tyr

Mannaz is mostly used to represent a man, or woman, for that matter. It can be used in a spell as a representation of a specific person. Used with Ansuz, it can be used to enhance someone's intelligence. Maybe even add Ehwas and Raido to it to strengthen it as a bind rune. It can be used for career and group ventures.

Phonetic value-M

Laguz: meaning- lake, water

God/Goddess- Niord, Nerthis, Ran, Freyja

Laguz is used to represent the element of water or the moon at times. Good for lost things or memories or truth. Good for emotional problems or illness. It may help women with their reproductive cycle.

Phonetic value-L

Inguz: meaning- the God Frey

Inguz is used to represent the earth at times. It can represent all four elements. A rune of growth and fertility. Inguz can be used instead of a circle to encompass other runes in general. It may help with fitness and overall well-being. It can be used to "box" something in or nurture it before letting it go.

Phonetic value-NG

Othila: meaning- inherited land

God/Goddess- Odin

Othila is used for any spell in which land, money, or inheritance is involved. It can help finish a project or strengthen a family. Can invoke Odin as the Wanderer or teacher.

Phonetic value-O

Dagaz: meaning- Day.

God/Goddess-Heimdal

Dagaz can be used for gradual change or a positive outcome when the spell involved is about daily things. It can be used to motivate. It may help in general healing. It is also used to hide things from view.

Phonetic value-D

RUNIC DIVINATION

*Just a quick reference you might want to read

There are lots of books on divination. Runes and tarot seem to be the favorites. So, I'll not go too deep into this subject. Like tarot, you can draw runes and place them in specific positions that denote what they represent...past, present, and future. Etc.

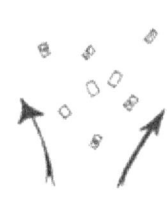

Free casting, I believe, is the way to go. Although a rune, 1, quickie, or the 3-rune pick works well, free casting takes a little more intuition. It requires the reader to be at the top of their game.

1. Have the person you're reading for hold all the runes for a moment.

2. Take the runes back from them and cast them in front of you.

3. Remove the unturned runes.

4. Look at the remaining runes. The runes in the center are the central theme unless a specific rune shape stands out to you.

5. The runes on the outside are forces trying to get in, things already passed (runes closest to the reader),

possible future (runes furthest away

from reader), etc.

6. The reader must decide which is the past and which is the future.

7. Take care to read groups of runes close together as closely associated in meaning.

8. you can also have the person pull a single rune to represent the overall theme of the reading.

*Getting as many books as possible, and doing as much reading as you can on this subject is paramount. The runes speak to each of us in slightly different ways. Try using reminder cards to help yourself along the way. Learn games to help attune yourself with the runes. Maybe bake cookies in the shape of each one (only one a day).

ᚠ Abundance, wealth, gains in riches or possessions, luck in general, of course, agriculture, and the ability to create these things.

ᚢ Challenge, rite, and initiation could represent accrual tests/time of strength, maybe even opportunities or risks.

ᚦ Disruptive, threatening, painful, possible misfortune could represent a specific problem or a shadow on the subconscious, maybe a blockage in creative energies.

ᚨ How we express ourselves, matters regarding messages or correspondence, wisdom, intelligence, or the lack thereof in a problem, blessed by Odin.

ᚱ Journey, adventure, movement, and momentum, all of which may be physical or spiritual.

ᚲ Warmth, friendship, love, illumination of a subject.

ᚷ Gift(s), the act of exchange, generosity, agreements, contracts, settlements.

ᚹ Joy, pleasure, bliss, fulfillment.

ᚺ Disruption, delay, frustrating times, difficulties, "Hail of destruction," possible past events.

ᚾ Hardship, constraints, suffering, inability to act, possible karmic challenge, general need, guilt (moral)

ᛁ Stasis, stagnant, emotional shutdown or frigidity, stopped in your tracks, frustration, no immediate solution, the universe has halted you for a reason.

ᛃ Year, annual, gain from efforts, fruitful conditions, reaping what you sow, the return of something.

ᛇ Major transition or change, life, and death (maybe symbolic), a possible state of suspension.

ᛈ Secrets, hidden talents, things not manifested, having something gained from our ancestors, possible birth of a child, female properties.

ᛉ Protection, defense, shielding, etc.

ᛋ Victory, success, higher self.

ᛏ Conflict, confrontation, and possible fight with the opposition are something you must face head-on, all of which could be personal, legal, social, political, etc.

ᛒ Inception of a new phase, fertility, purification, possible birth, new relationship, new project, growth, creativity.

ᛗ Movement, mobility, need to move literally, spiritual movement, astral movement.

ᛗ Specific person, people in general, the person asking questions (the runes around will denote this).

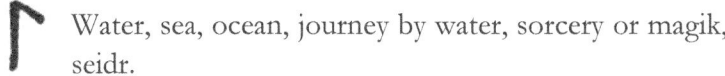 Water, sea, ocean, journey by water, sorcery or magik, seidr.

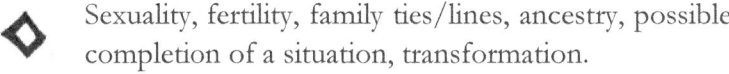 Sexuality, fertility, family ties/lines, ancestry, possible completion of a situation, transformation.

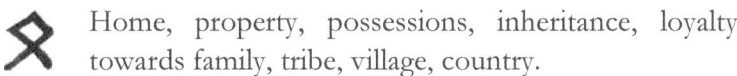 Home, property, possessions, inheritance, loyalty towards family, tribe, village, country.

Day, earthly blessings, spiritual enlightenment, a catalyst initiating change, beginning of the next cycle.

*You could also try enhancing your state of mind and see what you get. Maybe burn "Oracle Sage," inhale and read. Be careful, and only use something you investigated exceptionally well.

*I didn't put the names with the symbols for one reason...if you don't know the name, you shouldn't be casting quite yet. *Stay with a steady theme for the entire read.

Odin! Thee I call thee, I invoke in thine aspect of Grimnir, the hooded one!

By the Norns' nail, by Bragi's tongue, By Sleipnir's jaw teeth, and the neb of the night owl

By blood, by bone, by kinsfolk gone before, Thee I call thee I invoke!"

Come, All-Father, into this circle To bless and consecrate the casting that is to be performed!"

TROLL RUNES

Which runes are written, and in which order and number are important. The sequence in which the runes fall determines the outcome. Not just for Troll Runes.

*Quick Reference:

1. meaning/power of the rune

2. servitude/bondage

3. trigger number to activate (minor invocation)

4. annoyance/discomfort

5. satisfaction/success

6. inconvenience, or unwelcome

7. sexual matters

8. trigger, completion, strength (major invocation)

9. full completion, even greater than 8."

*Now that that's out of the way, let's move on to the TROLL RUNES!

The Troll Rune is Thurisaz. Not by itself, of course, but when written three times.

Now, we add the runes you wish to follow. Remember, Thurisaz, in this form, bastardizes any rune that follows. So, we'll use the extreme opposite of each rune...

RUNE	OPPOSITE	RUNE	OPPOSITE
Fehu	Poverty	Eiwaz	Loss of skills
Uruz	Loss of Strength	Pertho	Female lust/ weakness

Thurisaz	Power	Algiz	Defenselessness
Ansuz	Cursing	Sowulo	Scorching heat, ultimate defeat
Raido	Storms	Teiwas	Injustice, defeat
Kennaz	Filth	Berkana	Sterility(women)
Gebo	Loss, meanness	Ehwaz	Uncertainty

Wunjo	Frenzy, sadness	Mannaz	Adversity
Hagalaz	Floods	Laguz	Drought
Nauthiz	Disablement	Inguz	Sterility (men), lust
Isa	Treachery	Othila	Loss of family money
Jera	Famine, shortage	Dagaz	Night, darkness

DELFINO'S RUNIC SEALS

*All seals must be contained within a circle that controls their actions. (I.e., Always active or tap three times to unleash) This is, of course, for the safety of all.

Invincibility in battle and in life:

Note: As you write the runes, try chanting their names. This will charge each rune as you do so. Each rune has its own sound.

Fear and despair in my enemies:

Note: Here, I created a seal containment phrase for safety.

I would only launch this seal when in serious need. These types of things can backfire if you're not careful.

*Always double-check your work and be sure the right runes, or the ones you chose, are in the right positions and there is the right number of them.

Great things always:

These are just some seals. You can create any type you might need. Just remember to follow the meanings of the runes and the number of times you write each one. These are all extremely important...be very careful!!!

OTHER SCRIPTS

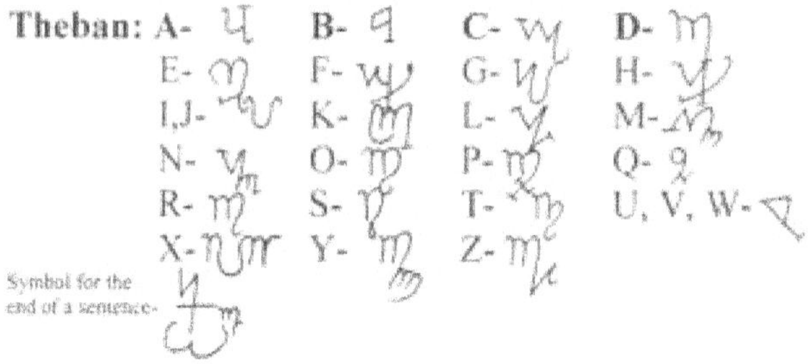
Theban:
A-
B-
C-
D-
E-
F-
G-
H-
I,J-
K-
L-
M-
N-
O-
P-
Q-
R-
S-
T-
U, V, W-
X-
Y-
Z-
Symbol for the end of a sentence-

Ogam:
b l f s n h d t c q ea ia
Ae m g ng st r a o u e i

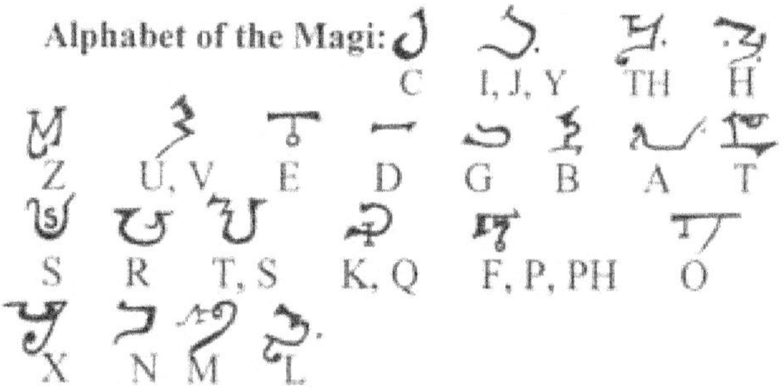
Alphabet of the Magi:
C
I, J, Y
TH
H
Z
U, V
E
D
G
B
A
T
S
R
T, S
K, Q
F, P, PH
O
X
N
M
L

Danish Runes

F U TH A R K H N I A S T B M L R

Swedish-Norse Runes

F U TH A R K H N I A S T B M L R

Ruthwell-

Vienna-

Thames-

F U TH O R C G W H N I J E P Z S

Scandinavian Runes

Ruthwell-

Vienna-

Thames-

T B E M L NG O D A AE Y EA K K G ST

Anglo-Saxon Runes

A B C D E F G H IJ K L M N O Q P R S

T U V W X Y Z NG GH EA AE OE TH

Seax-wica Runes

CHAPTER 5:

POTIONS

Here is my personal recipe for Mugwort tea that works like a charm. If dreams are what you want, then dreams are what you'll get. I also included a non-alcoholic and an alcoholic version of the "Elixir of Life" ...mead.

*Please remember to consult your doctor first before ingesting anything in this book.

DREAM POTION: DELFINO'S MUGWORT TEA

*Your last dream before you wake up tends to be the most significant.

Mugwort is a member of the Artemisia family, a botanical name in honor of the Greek lunar deity Artemis. Mugwort stimulates the production of dreams. It also enhances clarity, vividness, and your ability to remember dreams.

To Start:

1. 1/2 tablespoon Mugwort (production of dreams)

2. 1/4 tablespoon ginseng (cleansing)

3. 1/2 tablespoon catnip (relaxing dreams)

4. 1/4 tablespoon cinnamon (taste)

5. 2 tablespoons honey (taste)

6. 1/2 tablespoon ginkgo leaves (memory)

*Add as much honey and any type of real tea you might need for taste. You might have to adjust the amount of all the herbs for effect. Steep the herbs in boiling water for at least 10 min.

*All measurements are per cup...be careful!

*No milk...it changes the composition of the herbs.

*<u>Consult your doctor first.</u>

BEAUTIFUL MEAD

Non-alcoholic:

1. Boil 2 Quarts of water

2. Add 2 1/2 lbs. honey and 1/2 cup of

3. lemon zest (lemon peels)

Then, one tablespoon strong tea

4. 2 egg whites already beaten

5. Boil all contents for 10 min.

6. Let cool overnight (6-7 hours)

7. Strain and chill

Alcoholic:

1. Boil 2 quarts of water

2. Add 21/2-3 lbs. of honey

3. Add 1/2 cup of lemon zest (or 3

4. Add 1 - 1 1/2 tablespoons strong tea (or 11/2 teaspoons tartaric acid)

5. Add 1/2 cup fresh fruit (or 1/4 teaspoon grape tannin)

6. Skim any froth off the top as it boils

7. Let it cool and pour it into a glass bottle overnight

8. Next day, pour through a strainer into gallon fermentation

9. Add yeast into 1/2 cup of hot water and let stand 10 min.

19. Stir into mead (yeast)

11. Put it into a moderate temp. Dark place and put on the fermentation lock

12. You might like to put something underneath it to catch the foam off during the 1st few days

13. After the mead clears for a few days, pour the mead through the strainer again and top off the bottle with distilled water.

14. Check every so often for sediment.

15. when a month goes by without sediment, you can bottle the mead

16. Drink, or let age three months...it's up to you.

*When you add fruit/grapes, the mead will mature more rapidly. It could be ready in 3 months. This is the reason for the 1/4 teaspoon grape tannin. Malic acid, tartic acid, and grape tannin can all be bought at your local winery. You may want to discuss with them the recipe I've just given. Also, thanks be to the *"Brewers Guild of the Asatru Free Assembly"* for helping people brew great mead.

*Aegir (a-gear) "Ale Brewer), the Vana-God of the sea.

CHAPTER 6:

ANIMAL ALLIES

I've thrown in a quick history lesson on cats for your reading pleaser, as well as a ritual on how to find your Fetch, consecrate, and protect them. Looking after our helpers and our protectors is extremely important. They make magikal work go so smoothly for us.

A CAT'S HISTORY

*Considering that cats have been persecuted as much as we have been, I figured I'd put a little history lesson in here!

Cats were domesticated in the "Fertile Crescent" which starts in Egypt and stretches on towards Turkey and surrounding areas.

As the only animal that seems to have domesticated itself, they are completely self-reliant. It appears they first came out of the forest to get to the rodents from our villages and farms. In return, we feed them for help. They are still one of a few domestic animals that go Feral when left alone.

In the Middle Ages during the Inquisition, as witches were hunted down...so too were cats, any cats. Due to this, the rodent population thrived. Of course, we know what came next...the "Black Death". There just weren't enough cats left to stop it. The Christians' and Catholics' hatred for us almost wiped out the human race.

It was, in part, pictures of Freyja with her 2 cats, Honey and Amber, that was recognized as a typical witch. It didn't help that cats are nocturnal and tend to have unusual personalities. They come when they want...not when we call.17 So, love your cat... they know our pain.

FINDING YOUR FAMILIAR

*This may need to be done over a nine-day period

1. Find yourself a place of solitude where no one will disturb you outside.

*Cast circle, Call fairies, Call the Grey Wanderer, Call the Quarters.

2. You could do a light fast the whole time; just take a little food and a little water. (No meats, no sweets, no treats)

3. Burn specific incense for this rite, what you would normally use for visions or vision quests and wait patiently for your answer. (Oracle sage-sandalwood-hemlock- henbane-parsley-cinnamon- Dragon's blood)

*Now meditate on the reason you're here...what is it you're looking for? What do you want to accomplish?

(Remember not to be too specific; the cosmos will send you what you really need)

*Now, just be responsive to your surroundings. The messenger may appear to you in the open, or they may be a little more elusive than that.

Incantation: (while you meditate)

"Fetch, of self-reveal to me What it is I need to see. Keep me safe and out of harm; we are one; now come to me!"

*Close your circle when finished.

* You could also use a type of "stimulant" for the meditation. Just be careful!

FAMILIAR CONNECTION

*A familiar or "Fetch" is an individual creature with which you have specifically established a psychic bond. It's an animal, usually, that lives with you...like the cat that's always by you. Or, maybe it's the dog that only sleeps in the room with you.

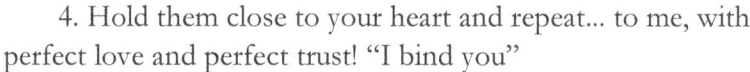

1. Create a ritual circle as usual

2. Burn dragon's blood at all 4 quarters

3. Sit inside the circle with your familiar

4. Hold them close to your heart and repeat... to me, with perfect love and perfect trust! "I bind you"

5. Kiss their head as you repeat it

6. Take some of their hair, or feathers, etc. Place in cauldron for later.

*If your familiar is a cat, sprinkle dried catnip inside the circle and let them play for a while.

Protection of your familiar:

1. Take a picture of them

2. Cut out their face in the shape of a heart

3. On the back draw Algiz for protection

4. Cleans it in dragon's blood or sage

5. Now ask whichever God/Goddess you wish to protect them

6. Tape the hair, feathers, etc. (from before) to the back

7. Keep with your altar at all times

*I call on Freyja for this. Maybe even keep a rowan branch near it on the altar to protect against malevolent magik.

*I also tend to own animals of the opposite sex. I seem to bond better with them.

*Bygul (bee-gool), "bee-gold" or honey, and Tryegul (tree-gool), "tree-gold" or amber, were the names of Freyja's 2 cats that pull her chariot.

Havamal-Stanza-158

"I know a thirteenth if I shall pour water Over your warrior;

He will not fall though he goes into battle; before swords, he will not sink!"

The runes to chant for this spell are...

CHAPTER 7:

RITES AND RITUAL

Being a book for the modern Viking, I felt it imperative to put in things for day-to-day life. Marriages and creating offspring are staples of life then and now. Astral Travel and Shamanic Transformation are updated versions of the old ways of our people.

As for the initiation...you must be serious. Dedicating your life to the craft is no small task. It means being ridiculed by others and blamed for things you didn't do. Initiation is your rebirth into a new life of learning about nature and the energies around you. It also means helping those who are in need of help, even if they hate you after.

*Belladonna and Hemlock are extremely poisonous and can harm or kill you. Any and all poisonous herbs in this book are for reference only. They were part of the original writings of the past. Likewise, some of the herbs here are skin irritants and may cause rashes or worse. Please be careful and speak with a professional if needed.

INITIATION

(Solitary)

*This can be used as an initiation ritual or a re-dedication ritual.

*Cast the circle, call Fairies, Grey Call Wanderer, the Call quarters...

1. Light a yellow candle and place it at the East, say... GUNGNIR (GOONG-NEAR): "I give my honor to 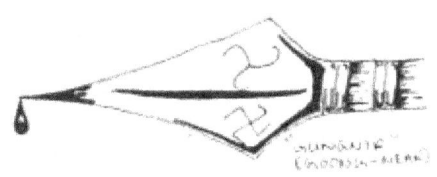 the quarters and the Shinning Ones, my Gods. Hail Odin! Hail Odin!"

2. Light a red candle and place it at the South, say... "I give my honor to the quarters and the Shinning Ones, my Gods. Hail Dvalin! Hail Odin!"

3. Light a blue candle and place it at the West, say... "I give my honor to the quarters and the Shinning Ones, my Gods. Hail Dain! Hail Odin!"

4. Light a green candle and place it at the North, say... "I give my honor to the quarters and the Shinning Ones, my Gods. Hail Asvind! Hail Odin!"

5. Stand before the altar and the symbols of the Gods, say... "Hail Odin, All-Father,

Bringer of wisdom, knowledge, and victory. Bring me together with our people, That I may know your strength and ancient ways. Show me honor,

And how to prosper in your name. Hail Odin! Hail
Odin!'

*Meditate for a couple of mins.

"Hail Thor, Thunderer.

Bringer of power and safety.

Bring me together with our people,
That I may know your protection and
compassion. Show me honor,

And how to prosper in your name.

Hail Thor! Hail Thor!"

*Meditate for a couple of mins.

"Hail Freyja, the Beautiful. Bringer of love and lust.

Bring me together with our people,

That I may know your beauty and passion.

Show me honor,

And how to prosper in your name.

Hail Freyja! Hail Freyja!"

*Meditate for a couple of mins.

6. Raise your arms to the sky, say...

"Oh, Great Shinning Ones, I call to you. It is I, your
ancestor. I am your kith and kin. Here and now, I honor you.
As I am part of Gaia and Middle Earth, I am part of you. The
plants and animals, the lakes and seas, the trees and stones are
all my brothers and sisters. We are all built of the same stars
and dust...the same spark of divinity. I am of you, and you are
of me. So, mote it be!"

*Drink from your horn or goblet.

7. Lower arms, say...

"Grant me my desires, that I may rejoice in all things I am one with. Show me the love and life that radiates from you into all beings and things. I will protect and nurture the spark of the divine within myself and our people. I will give my word sparingly and adhere to it like iron. I will never neglect my mate or children. For love is the law and bond of our people. These things I will honor always!"

*Drink from your horn or goblet.

8. Kiss your right palm, then hold it high, say...

stand before you in

"My ancestors, kith and kin, I perfect love and perfect trust. Here and now, I dedicate myself and my life to you and your honor. I will always be honest with myself and others. As you protect and defend me, so too will I try to protect and defend our people. You are my life, and I abide by the principles of the "Rede of Honor."

Hail Odin! Hail Thor! Hail Freyja!"

*Drink from your horn or goblet.

9. Slowly pour the remainder of the liquid from your horn, say...

"Let my blood pour from my body like the mead from this horn should I ever turn my back on the Shinning Ones. Should my life force drain from me if I ever harm our people in malice or break your trust? It would be better to fall on my sword than to cast aside the love and trust of the High Ones. Here and now, I am reborn through the cauldron of rebirth. The love of the Gods embraces me so that I may honor them in all that I do. Hail Odin! Hail Thor! Hail Freyja!"

10. Dip your forefinger into the water in the West, and make the sign of the solar cross over your 3rd eye, say...

"As I continue to learn the craft, I choose the name

. Know my name, Great Ones, that I may honor you. Be in me, of me, and with me always.

Hail Odin! Hail Thor! Hail Freyja!"

*Meditate on your new name (tell no one)

11. Face the altar, raise your arms, say...

"Thank you, Great Ones,

For being here with me.

May I always honor you,

And our people to the fullest.

With your spark,

I will continue my work.

Hail Odin! Hail Thor! Hail Freyja!"

*Close circle; your rite has ended.

*In the craft, we take on many names. There are the names we use inside our coven and then there is the name you use by yourself. The one you use by yourself is for your own ears and the Gods only. This is so no one can cast spells in your direction with great ease or effect.

*Hugginn (hoog-in) "thought" and Munnin (moon-in) "memory" are Odin's giant ravens.

*Geri (gir-ee), "greedy," and Freki (frisk-ee), and "voracious" are Odin's 2 great wolves.

67

*Toothgnasher and Toothgrinder are Thor's giant goats who pull his chariot. They can be eaten and brought back to life.

*Hildisvini (hill-dee-sveen-ee) is Freyja's "Battle Pig"

*Havamal-Stanza-145

"Better not to pray than to sacrifice too much. One gift always calls for another;

Better not dispatch than to slaughter too much. So Thund carved before the history of nations, Where he rose up when he came back! "20

TOAST, BOAST AND OATH

(Solitary)

*This is a basic oath ceremony for the New Year.

*Cast Circle, Call Fairies, Call Grey Wanderer, Call the Quarters.

1. Stand before your altar and hold your hands up to the sky, say...

"By the runes carved on Sleipnir's jaw-teeth,

Hear me, Odin, All father.

It is me, your ancestor.

I call upon you to hear this oath!"

"By your one hand of justice, Hear me, Tyr, Oath Taker.

It is me, your ancestor.

I call upon you to hear this oath.

"By the Magik that resides in Brisingamen,

Hear me, Freyja, Vana-Goddess.

It is me

, your ancestor.

I call upon you to hear this oath!"

"By the power that flows through Mjollnir,

Hear me, Thor, Protector of man.

It is me, your ancestor.

I call upon you to hear this oath!

Hail Odin! Hail Tyr! Hail Freyja! Hail Thor!"

2. Pick up your drinking horn or goblet, and hold it up high in your right hand, facing the North, saying...

"By all the Gods and Goddesses of the lovely realms,

I stand here proud and strong before you.

May my blade be sharp?

May my belly be full? And may my bed be warm!"

*Drink from your horn or goblet.

3. Raise it up again and say a Toast. It could be to fallen heroes and ancestors, or it could be to someone else's good deeds.

*Drink from your horn or goblet, and then pour a little on the ground.

4. Raise it up again and say a Boast. This is something you've done over the last year last you can boast about...good deeds, Good fights, etc.

*Drink from your horn or goblet, and then pour a little on the ground.

5. Raise it up again and say an Oath. This is a promise to the Gods, which is much more serious than a new-years resolution. An oath must never be broken, or it will affect your Hamingja or karma.

* Drink from your horn or goblet, and then pour a little on the ground.

*Meditate on your oath for a few minutes.

6. Replace the Drinking horn, or goblet, on the altar

7. Stand facing the North with arms raised up to the sky, say...

"Like the sun rises and sets each day,

I will adhere to my oath like iron.

I will never faultier in my quest,

I will never stumble in my deeds.

Hear, and now I pledge to my Gods,

I will honor them in all that I do.

Hail Odin! Hail Tyr! Hail Freyja! Hail Thor!"

*The Oath has been said now to end with the circle open to represent the beginning of the new year and things to come.

HAND-FASTENING

*This is a marriage/binding ritual

*Godi- priest   **Godia- priestess**

Women are to be revered highly, for they are the givers of life. They are in no way property, as the major religions would have you believe. They are the avatars of the Goddess herself. Hand-fasting is the heathen version of marriage. Traditionally, it's renewed each year.

The bride should wear a simple dress, with a veil of her choice, maybe a crown, and a jewel, brochure, or rune ornament to symbolize Brisingamen, Freyja's magical necklace.

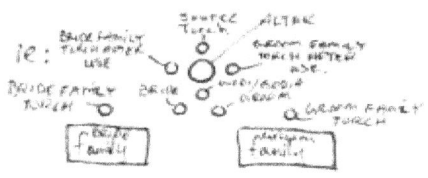

The groom should wear something simple but formal. The best-man should hold the groom's sword at his side until the groom has need of it.

*You will also need a red ribbon on the altar for the binding itself.

Hopefully done outside, the area could look like this...

The family torches are placed at the front of the family seating area, unlit at first.

1. One of the groom's family members walks him to the altar, carrying the family torch. Together, they use the source torch to light their torch, and it's placed on the right of the altar. The family member then returns to the seating area.

2. One of the bride's family members walks her to the altar, carrying the family torch. Together, they use the source torch to light their torch, and it's placed on the left of the altar. The family member then returns to the seating area.

3. The Godi/ Godia says...

"We are gathered here on this beautiful day/night to witness the hand-fasting of these two who profess their love to each other."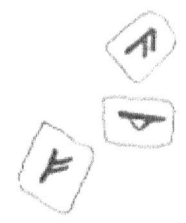

 4. The Godi/ Godia raises their arms and says...

"We call upon Odin, the All-Father,

To grant us wisdom in our choices. We call upon Thor, the red-bearded thunderer, to grant us strength to endure.

We call upon Freyja, the beautiful,

To grant us love and understanding. Hear our words as we speak them in truth!"

"We also invoke the great Goddess Var,

She hears the vows of men and women. And, Tyr, the great one-handed God of justice,

So, he may hear our oaths!"

5. After a short pause...Godi/ Godia says...

"Bring in the Hammer,

So that the Gods may consecrate,

And bless this binding!"

6. Thor's Hammer, Mjollnir,
is brought forth and given to the Godi/ Godia.

"Kneel to receive the blessings of the Gods!"

7. Both bride and groom kneel in front of Godi/ Godia.

8. The Hammer is touched to the head of the groom, Godi/ Godia says...

"By all the Gods, you are blessed!"

9. The Hammer is touched to the head of the bride, Godi/ Godia says...

"By all the Gods, you are blessed!"

10. Godi/ Godia prompts both to rise and says...

"I ask you, here in front of the Gods and our people, to give that which symbolizes your love to each other. Always to protect and care for one another!"

11. The best man hands the groom his sword, and the groom places its blade down, kneels facing the bride, and offers the handle to her, saying...

"My love, I oath my heart and soul to you.

Always to be at your service.

As my blade is strong, so will be my love. As its edge is sharp, so will my heart be strong. Accept this symbol of my oath to you!"

11. The bride takes the sword and touches it to her lips, kissing it and then saying...

"I accept your oath to me,

In perfect love and perfect trust!"

13. The bride then gives the sword back to the groom, the groom kisses the sword as well, and he

75

returns it to the best man. (groom stays kneeling)

14. The bride then removes her jewel/broche/rune and holds it out to the groom with both hands, saying...

"My love, I oath my heart and soul to you.

Always to be at your service.

As this jewel/broach/rune is beautiful, so will my heart be strong.

As its value endures, so will my love for you.

Accept this symbol of my oath to you!"

15. The groom takes the jewel/broche/rune and touches it to his lips, kissing it and saying...

"I accept your oath to me,

In perfect love and perfect trust!"

16. Then the groom gives the jewel/broche/rune back to the bride and stands. They both face the Godi/Godia.

17. The Godi/Godia says...

"You who are here to be bound,

Hear me now.

May you accomplish great things in life. May you love each other with perfect trust. May your love be ever-lasting like the stars.

May your hearts be solid like the stones of Gaia. With these oaths, you gain the greatest treasure...love!"

18. Godi/Godia pauses and then says...

"Do you desire_____ forsaking all others?" (Groom answers)

"Do you desire_____ forsaking all others?"
(Bride answers)

19. Godi/Godia hands the bride and groom their rings and

"As a symbol of this hand-fasting,

Place these rings on each other's hands!"

20. Now, the Godi/Godia takes the red ribbon off the altar and wraps it around the bride's left hand and the groom's right hand, saying...

"In the name of the Gods,

May you know only prosperity and good fortune.

Now seal the oath with a kiss!

21. They kiss and then turn to face the gathering.

22. Godi/Godia says...

May the Gods be with you always, Blessed be!"

*The Hand-Fastening is done.

SHAMANIC TRANSFORMATION

"Transformation Oil": Crush with a mortar and pestle the following herbs, Hemlock-Henbane-Parsley-Cinnamon-Dragon's Blood-Rowan- Belladonna

*Warning: This was originally a salve, not oil. Either way, this is only for reference. Most of these herbs will either irritate your skin or poison you.

*Belladonna and Hemloch can kill you!!

The "Berserkers" were the fiercest warriors in battle. They did similar rituals for initiation as well as to prepare for battle. They believed that during battle, they took the form of bears or wolves, possessing their strengths and powers. They also believe that they became impervious to both sword and fire. I think they also dabbled in some types of "stimulants" as well. This ritual can be used to become any animal you wish at any time...not just for battle.

*Study the animal you wish to become...how they move, what sounds they make. Etc. If it's possible, dress in their fur or feathers or just paint your skin to look like them. (Do not kill this animal just for this reason!)

*Create an animal ally altar for the spirit you wish to invoke. Use pictures, figurines, representations, etc. Offer some sort of food as well. The altar can be similar to your regular one; just make it separate and dedicate it to your ally only.

*Open circle as usual, Call Fairies, Call the Grey Wanderer, Call Quarters.

1. Light candles on ally altar, one for the animal and one for Odin, say...

"Odin, shaman of the North.

Giver of runes and magik,

Here is my call.

Grant me your gift of transformation. Let me share in your abilities, That I may do my work.

Hear me, All-father.

Hail Odin! Hail Odin!"

*Meditate on that for a few minutes.

2. With arms raised, imagine the animal's spirit above you, facing the same way.

3. Now, imagine the spirit settling down over the top. Identify the animal's attributes and charge it with energy.

4. Look through the spirits' eyes as your own and project your being into the animal, say...

"I invoke your spirit of

Here is my call.

Be here with me, in me, and of me.

Share your energy with me.

So, mote it be!"

*Remember you will not actually change form, but your spiritual energy will. People with the sight may see you as the animal. Other animals will perceive you as the spirit.

*You may also cause yourself to astral project as one with the animal. This will leave your body sitting on the

ground or lying down unconscious. Now you can do some traveling. For this, I would make sure you're in a safe place to do it. You leave your body exposed otherwise.

*Odin can also give one of these 3 frenzies, madnesses, or transformations...the warrior in battle, the seer in trance, and the poet in creativity.

Trance through chanting and drumming:

In Northern Shamanism, the emphasis is on sound. Chanting and drumming are combined with breathing and the human heartbeat. 2 types of "work" can be done through this. One is outward work such as spells and such. The 2nd is inward, such as reflection and divination.

Drumming is excellent for creating altered states. Find a drum that calls to you. Go out and find something handmade. You first need to become comfortable with your new friend. By rhythmic drumming, one can find one's own "spiritual tone" ...the tone that releases one's magical energy. When drumming, listen for other sounds joining in with you. Experiment to see what works for you.

Chanting is also very useful. Songs and chants can be used for all sorts of work.

Try your own chants or use the rune's names individually or together to achieve the desired effect. This does work quite well. Again, experiment and see what works.

*All of these can be done sober or with an added "stimulant" to enhance your mood. Always be careful. Maybe record your work to better understand how it all went. You could also record something to be played in the background while you "work."

*Freyja Aswynn has a great CD for chants called "Songs of Yggdrasil." Every person listening to this CD will learn how to chant properly.

*Keep an eye open for any spirit guides that show up! *If you do record your work, do so ASAP! Memories can become quickly altered.

Havamal-Stanza-155

"I know a tenth one if I see demons Playing up in the air;

I can bring it about that they can't make their way

back

To their own shapes,

To their own spirits! "23

The runes to chant for this spell are...

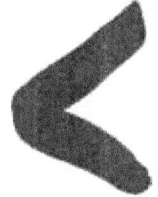

ASTRAL TRAVEL

Most believe the soul is tethered to the body spiritually, so be confident that you will always return. However, this is never to be taken lightly. For some it may take years to achieve, and some gain this ability right away. Some even achieve it at the start then struggle soon after. Take your time; this is not something that should be rushed. Allow it to happen on its own.

DO NOT FORCE IT!

 *You may want to choose incense to burn to facilitate your memory's connection to this specific work. Or, mix traditional incense...cinnamon-mugwort-sandalwood

1. Lie down; relax; shut your eyes

2. Breathe deeply

3. Repeat to yourself out loud 3 times...

"First, I think, then I fly.

I will return; I shall not die!"

4. Visualize yourself standing at the end of your bed, exactly as it is, looking at yourself

*Once achieved, the universe is yours to explore!

Warning: Never do this when intoxicated, on sleeping pills, or extremely tired!

Havamal-Stanza-155

"I know a tenth one if I see demons Playing up in the air;

I can bring it about that they can't make their way back

To their own shapes, To their own spirits! "24

The runes to chant for this spell are...

BABY MAKER

"Fertility Bag": Take a medicine bag and fill it with any combo of these numbering between 3 and 6...

Sea shells-egg shells-blood stone-moon stone- quarts-small doll-snake figurine-black cohosh- serpentaria-rattle snake root-rattle snake

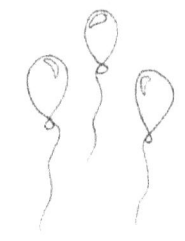

master-adder' stonguerowan-snake weed-basil lemon balm- parsley-fairy charms-Astarte oil-hawthorn leaves, twigs, bark,

etc.

*Any combo of these should do the trick. Of course, the more you put into something, the better it turns out. All snake references are because snakes used to be considered a fertility animal before the Christians bastardized it.

Astarte oil:

- Essential oil of coriander
- Essential oil of jasmine
- Essential oil of myrrh
- Essential oil of petitgrain or neroli
- Rose Attar25

*Blend all ingredients with sweet almond and jojoba oils.

Maybe add rose petals.

*Essential oils can be dangerous to a woman already pregnant. If you know for sure you're not pregnant, rub it on your thighs, on the inside, to enhance the possibility of conception. Otherwise, only use this for ritual and magikal purposes.

1. Go out and find a Hawthorn tree. Collect any parts of it that are lying on the ground, leaves, twigs, etc. Promise the fairies you'll set up an offering in the new baby's room when they come. Hawthorns are very sacred to fairies. You could also make a small doll and tie it to the tree with a pink/red ribbon as an offering to the tree for its help. (Trees have been considered good for fertility, especially the ones that bare fruit, nuts, and birch)

2. Set up an altar in your bedroom near the bed. Add your medicine bag to the altar along with nuts, fruit, Astarte oil, and any of the herbs from the list above and a purple/pink candle. Cleanse the whole room as you would your ritual space. Place living roses and lavender around the room. Add any of these...

Jasmine-lotus-moon flowers

3. Carve the runes for the baby and any other runes needed to promote conception.

4. Place the candle in the cauldron you rub Astarte oil on it.

5. Light a candle and Call Fairies into your room.

6. Write on a piece of

paper your desires.

7. Meditate on the paper for a moment. Then, light on fire, saying...

"As I light this now on fire,

Take my wishes higher and higher.

We want a baby to have and to hold,

We'll give them love and teach them secrets untold.

Freyja, my Goddess hear my plea,

I'll be a good parent, this you'll see!"

8. Let paper burn in a cauldron

9. Take the fertility botanicals you put on your altar and add a small amount of each to the cauldron.

10. Rub Astarte oil on the inside of your thighs and thank Freyja for being with you. Leave the candle burning.

11. Now go grab your mate and make love with a purpose

ground.

12. When you're done, bury all the cauldron contents in the

*After lovemaking, take a bowl of milk outside and leave it for the strays in the area. Maybe even leave some catnip, too.

*If you have a cat, give them a bowl of milk and speak with Freyja through the cat, explaining what you want. The cat may answer.

Havamal-Stanza-163

"I know an eighteenth which I shall never teach

To any girl or any man's wife

It's always better when just one person knows

It follows at the end of the spells

Except for that one woman whom my arms embrace

Or maybe my sister!"

The runes to chant for this spell are...

CHAPTER 8:

SPELLS AND INCANTATIONS

Here is my favorite section. Spells are nothing to play around with. It's very important to realize that even when you mean well, things can go wrong. And don't fool yourself one bit; you will be blamed. Humans as a race have not come so far down the path of enlightenment as we'd like to think. Ignorance and superstitions run ramped still today.

This is the biggest chapter for a reason...I spent the most time on it. After taking as much time as it did to write this, I didn't want to forget something important. Any and all the spells are tried and true, like the herbs in them. I only wrote down what I could verify personally. I referenced the spells right out of the Havamal and put them at the end of each of my own.

That being said, be careful. What works for one person might not work for another. Things might change, and you may need to re-arrange the Gods and ideas as you see fit. Take what you need and leave the rest.

It's also good to change parts and make it more personal anyway. Never do a spell exactly as it's written by someone else. You have to put something personal into it for it to work right. Even if it's only a word change in a rhyme or chant, go by feeling.

I try not to cast spells for people unless they ask me to. Even if they do, things could change due to an unfavorable outcome. The cosmos gives us what we need, not what we always want.

LOVE MAKER

"Magik Ring Spell": Done 1st to add to the strength; prepare this the day of the full moon. Then, leave it on the altar until the next full moon.

1. Use a simple gold ring or any ring available

2. Fill a chalice with spring water and add to it rose petals, tulips, basil, cinnamon, lilacs, catnip, or any item that means love to you.

3. Hang the ring just under the surface of the water using a pencil or something similar and a red/pink ribbon.

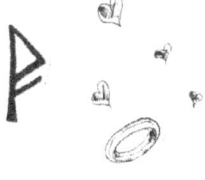

4. Draw a heart on red paper, cut it out, and draw on it the runes of your desires. Love- Victory- Gift- Joy- Need- Freyja-

5. On the back of the heart, write "True Love" in runes.

6. Place the chalice on top of the heart, on the altar, say...

"Divine love bless my sleep, my true love I shall keep!"

*ALWAYS REMEMBER THIS IS ALL WITH FREE WILL!

*On the night of the next full moon, set up as you would and cast a circle. Call Fairies, Call the Grey Wanderer, Call the Quarters, Invoke the Quarters.

1. Already having carved the runes on a candle representing "True Love Come To Me," Place the candle in your cauldron,

2. Light a candle and say...

"As this candle flame grows bright

And ever grows much higher,

Freyja, Goddess of love,

Bring me love's ever-burning fire

Then, as the flame does flicker low,

Finally, to depart.

Freyja, Goddess of love

Give me true love,

With an honest heart!"

*Shake Rattle, ring bell, 3 times

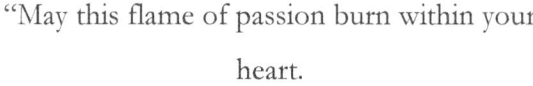

3. As the candle burns, sprinkle rose and lavender incense on it, and say...

"May this flame of passion burn within your

heart.

From me, you will not part!"

"I bind you to me; I'm all you'll see!"

*All work must be done with free will in mind.

4. Remove the ring from the chalice and hold it close to your heart, say...

"This ring is for true love; true love comes to me!

*Add any desires you might have now; be specific.

5. Place the ring on your Right ring finger or around your neck on a silk cord.

6. Take heart and hold it close to the candle flame, say...

"As this red heart glows in candlelight,

I draw you, lover, closer to me this night!"

7. Burn the heart with a candle and place it in the cauldron to burn. Burn it until it's gone, say...

"May our love burn undying!"

*Let the candle burn out on its own in a cauldron.

8. Place the cauldron's contents onto a red piece of paper. Add anything else you feel is special or needed. Fold the paper closed, tie it with a red or pink ribbon, seal it with wax, and carve on it.

"I drown in your love; you orbit my world!"

9. Using a dandelion gone to seed, hold it up, think of love, and blow your desires into the wind.

*Find a nice place outside to bury the package in Gaia, say...

"As I bury this in the soil, make it fast, not to toil!"

10. Gaze at the moon and say...

"Moon, beautiful moon.

Freyja, Goddess of love.

You look so beautiful to me as I see your face.

93

Let me look as beautiful to him/her as you do to me.

Our fate is sealed; we are as one.

So, mote it be, my work is done.

Hail Freyja! Hail Freyja!"

*Shake rattle, ring bell, 3 times.

*Now close the circle in perfect love and perfect trust.

Havamal-Stanza-161

"I know a sixteenth if I want to have all

A clever woman's heart and love play;

I can turn the thoughts of the white-armed woman

And change her mind entirely!"

The runes to chant for this spell are...

HEALING SPELL

"Talisman": Keep crystals on the altar during the rite to fill them with your intention. One or some of these crystals should do...

Alexandrite-jade-diamonds-loadstone-moon stone-pearls-blood stone-quartz

When you've completed the spell, put the stone(s) in a medicine bag with Rowan and the cloth talisman you created.

"Cloth Talisman": using the witches' sigil (wheel) is easy enough. Using a piece of cloth, draw the symbol you create using the wheel on it. Now add any other runes you wish.

"Moon Water": Take a clear bottle, put sea salt and water in it, and put it somewhere it will have direct moonlight from the next full moon. Use this to wash the affected area. If the area is inside, you must drink it, <u>but just a tiny sip.</u>

*Cast circle, Call Fairies, Call the Grey Wanderer, Call the Quarters, Invoke the Quarters.

1. Take the plain candle and carve the person's name on it in runes. Fill the rest of the space with the Algiz rune.

2. Take a picture of the person or paper with their name on it. Draw on the back the runes you wish...

Odin- Freyja- Protection- Strength- Victory-

3. Concentrate on the picture/paper with your intentions.

4. Set it on fire using a representation candle, say...

"Oh, Great Odin,

Wise Great Wanderer,

I call you here for your help.

Please take the pain away.

Give victory over this illness.

Hail Odin! Hail Odin!"

"Oh, Great Freyja,

Beautiful mother.

I call you here for your help.

Please take the pain away.

your magik to overcome illness.

Hail Freyja! Hail Freyja!"

Oh, Great Thor,

Red Bearded Thunderer.

I call you here for your help.

Please take the pain away.

Your strength to beat this illness.

Hail Thor! Hail Thor!"

5. Now add the herbs you've decided to use...

Rosemary-rowan-dittany of crete-lavender-thyme-corriander seed-willow-cinnamon-catnip

*You must add white sage.

6. After everything burns down before it hardens, add salt or sea salt to the cauldron to cleanse overall.

7. Give them the medicine bag talisman and wash the affected area with the moon water.

*Repeat as needed

Extra: White sage can be eaten to stimulate the immune system. You can also grind it to powder and rub it in the wound. Honey on an open wound works as well. It's a natural anti-bacterial. Natural honey is completely sterile. Sugar on a wound was used during the American Civil War.

Havamal-Stanza-147

"I know a second one which sons of men need,

Those who want to live as physicians!"

The runes to chant for this spell are...

CALL OF JUSTICE

*Warning: Remember, we're talking unbiased justice. You must be sure you're in the "right." Otherwise, stick to the "Spell of Persuasion" or "Hex Defender".

"Mojo Bag": make a small bag out of blue or purple material. Then, put the following herbs inside...

- Calendula-legal victories
- Slippery elm-protect against false testimony and accusations
- Rowan-protect against malevolent powers
- Dragon's Blood sage-purification energy
- High John-victory
- Cinnamon-Goddess
- Catnip-Freyja
- Sun Flower peddles male energy, courage, action

One drop of "Hex Smashing" oil (from the Hex Defender spell)

*Open circle, Call Fairies, Call Grey Wanderer, Call Quarters, Invoke Quarters.

1. Add one blue or purple candle to your cauldron

2. Dress the candle with runes for the word justice and any other runes you desire. (Teiwaz carved 3 times works quite well.)

3. You could rub "Hex Smashing" oil on the candle

"JUSTICE"

4. Place a photocopy of the justice card from any tarot deck under the cauldron

5. Take a moment to envision what you want, say...

"Odin, cloaked wanderer,

One-eyed rider,

With your ravens at your side,

Be with me here.

Horned God of the wild hunt,

Protect me from my enemies.

Grasper of fates and desires,

Twist my fate into success.

Hail Odin! Hail Odin!"

"Freyja, queen of the Shield Maidens,

Collector of half the slain.

Seidr, Goddess of Fate,

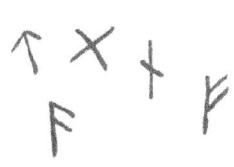

Whisper your spells in my ear.

Stand by my side,

Bind and chasten my enemies.

Protect your child,

In this time of need.

For my love for you is eternal,

Vana-Mother of all.

Hail Freyja! Hail Freyja!"

"Thor, protector of man,

Slayer of Giants.

Give me order and strength,

So, I may stand against my enemies.

Surround me with rightness,

Compel my fate towards good.

With your chariot,

Carry me on high.

Hail Thor! Hail Thor!"

"Tyr, keeper of oaths,

Bringer of justice.

With your one hand,

Lift me above my enemies.

Stand by me now,

In my time of need.

Bravest of the Gods,

Grant me my wish.

Hail Tyr! Hail Tyr!"

6. Add the same botanicals to the candle flame as you did to your "Mojo bag" (slowly to not put out the flame)

7. Add some crushed quartz to the cauldron for power, say...

"I want to rid myself of any who wish me ill.

Whose heart is cold as ice,

And only malice-filled.

No pain do I wish,

Or hatred do I make,

But free myself from harm,

For my own sake!"

8. Take a copy of the justice card out from under the cauldron.

9. On the back, write your desires and needs. Add the runes you put on the candle.

10. Meditate on this for a while, set it on fire with the candle flame in a cauldron, say...

"Tyr, God of justice,

My Viking spirit demands your help.

I require victory,

I need justice.

Transform this flame,

Into burning justice.

Your ancestor calls to you,

In my time of need.

Be with me, keeper of oaths,

With your one hand, create my fate.

Hail Tyr! Hail Tyr!"

11. Let the candle burn in a cauldron. Close your circle after the candle burns out.

12. Bury the cauldron contents somewhere nearby where the person you demand justice from will pass by or in your

backyard. When you bury it in Gaia, envision the person passing over it.

"As I bury this in the soil, make it work and never toil!"

Havamal-stanza-149

"I know a fourth one if men put

Chains upon my limbs;

I can chant so that I can walk away,

Fetters spring from my feet,

And bonds from my hands. "29

The runes to chant for this spell are...

SPELL OF PERSUASION

"Persuasion Oil": take mineral oil and add the following crushed herbs...

Passion flower-black cohosh root-licorice root-calamus root- cinnamon-sage-catnip-sunflower peddles-Dragon's blood- something personal

*Open circle, Call Fairies, Call the Grey Wanderer, Call the Quarters.

*This is all about persuasion, not control. We're just giving "free will" a little push.

*Place 8 of the swords card (or copy) on the altar. Then, put your cauldron on top of it with a candle inside.

*Carve what you want on the candle first.

1. On a piece of paper, write the name of the person you wish to persuade 9 times

2. Then write your name over top of each one 3 times

3. Roll up the paper and tie it with a string of your choosing

4. Think about what it is you want from them

5. Put it in the cauldron to burn, and say...

"Listen good and listen well; do as I say and as I tell!"

(Repeat 3 times)

Now, pull out the 8 swords from under the cauldron. Meditate on the opposite meaning of the card...

*8 of Swords: Bad news, imprisonment, crisis; the present cycle of adversity can be overcome if opportunity is grasped.

6. Place a drop of "Persuasion Oil" on the front of the card.

7. On the back, create a symbol or bind rune to counter the meaning of the card.

- Ansuz-communication and Odin
- Teiwaz-justice
- Wunjo-joy, success
- Raido-your "rights"
- Sowulo-victory, sun's power, reinforcement

*Could look like this...

*Rub the oil into the bind rune along with your connect you to the runes.

8. Remembering what you wish to happen, set the 8 of Swords on fire and place them in the cauldron, say...

"As I set this now of fire, take my wishes higher and higher!"

9. As the candle burns down, now is the time to add the herbs...

Passion flower-black cohosh root-licorice root-calamus root- cinnamon-catnip-sunflower peddles-sage-Dragon's blood- something personal

*Close circle, this rite has ended.

*Let them burn down and let them cool over night. In the morning or the next day, so out and put them somewhere the person will see, touch, or walk by.

Havamal-Stanza-153

"I know an eighth one, which is most useful

For everyone to know;

Where hatred flares up between the sons of warriors,

Then I can quickly bring settlement!"30

The runes to chant for this spell are...

DEATH & DYING

*To Ease Passing: Take pennyroyal and part of a rowan branch and grind as best you can. Place both in a medicine bag. Get (the dying) person you're doing the work for to wear it around their neck. Now turn all the mirrors I the house around so no one sees the Valkries or Odin when they come. The dying should never see their dead face.

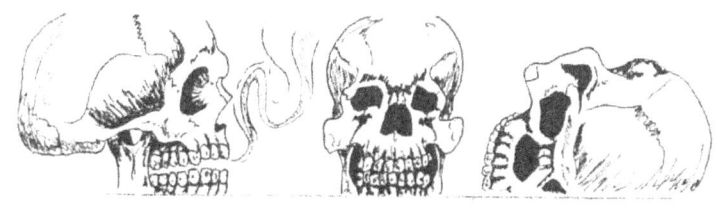

*You could create a lavender oil and sea salt solution to give to the mortician to clean their body ritually.

*After Death: place a figurine of one of the following psychopomps in the coffin or urn with them... Snake-crow/raven-dog-wolf-jackal

*Psychopomps are messengers for the dead. They tend to help a spirit cross over.

Now let go:

1. Morn for 9 days wearing the same clothes

2. Stay to yourself as best you can

3. On the 9th day, take a cleansing bath of rose oil

4. Submerge yourself at least 3 times

5. Get out of the bath and put on new clothes (just bought)

6. Write a letter to the loved one

7. Take old clothes outside along with the letter

8. Burn the clothes first

9. Read the letter out loud, then burn it too

10. Sweep the house with a ritual broom (bosom) to cleanse the area

11. Everything (dirt/debris) must go

12. Now, take the broom outside and burn it, or keep it as a summoning tool for that spirit. (Don't use until a year and a day has passed!)

*Now cast your circle, Call Fairies, Call the Grey Wanderer, Call the Quarters.

13. Put their picture on the altar. Then burn...

White sage-cinnamon-sandalwood-frankincense-benzoin

14. When you're ready, say...

"Now, at the end of _____ life,

I call upon the shining ones to hear me.

Odin the wise, Thor the strong,

And Freyja, the mother of us all.

Pleases come and claim _____ spirit.

Someone I have known and loved as kith and kin!"

"May _____ find peace during their transition.

May_____ help our kin when needed.

Like the Gods, our ancestors do!"

"May Odin himself choose you to reside in high Valhalla.

And may you be worthy of his choice.

Until Ragnarok, or the time of your rebirth!"

"May the mother Goddess Freyja send her Valkries to claim you.

May you see the inside of Folkvangr Hall!"

"Oh great, Shinning Ones,

Send the Shield Maidens to collect your ancestor.

And take them on high across the Rainbow Bridge!"

"We all meet again in the end.

So, until then,

May the Gods keep you well.

Hail Odin! Hail Thor! Hail Freyja!"

*Meditate on all this for as long as you like...then close the circle.

Havamal-Stanza-157

"I know a twelfth one if I see,

Up in a tree,

A dangling corpse in a noose;

I can carve and color the runes

That the man walks and talks with me!"

The runes to chant for this spell are...

SPIRIT SUMMONS

*Not to be taken lightly!** You should really know who or what it is you're summoning. Not knowing can lead to disaster or worse. Some spirits have their own smell or fragrance. The smell occurs when the spirit is near. Sometimes, your hair will stand up all over your body. Me, personally, my eyes well up. Banishing is also essential. If you do not do this right, the "guest" mat or could become a problem.

*Note:** Instead of demanding, you should invite or ask them to come without fear or contempt. Spirits are not above bribes or bargains (careful). This type of ritual is best done on Samhain.

"Spirit Summoning Oil": Crush and add to mineral oil the following...Benzoin-althaea-cinnamon-frankincense-rowan-sweetgrass-sage-grave yard dirt.

*Cast circle, Call Fairies, Call the Grey Wanderer, Call Quarters, Invoke Quarters.

1. Face the East

2. Announce your intentions

3. Ask to have God's protection. (Talk to them as you would to any family member, frank and honest).

4. Take a silver candle, carve the name of the spirit on it, and rub your "Spirit Summoning Oil" into it.

5. Light a candle and put it in your cauldron

6. Relax; begin putting any offerings and representations of the spirit on your altar.

*Offerings could be drinks, food, presents, etc. Anything you know the spirit likes.**

*Representations can be a picture, drawing, carving, or a doll. (A picture of Freyja and catnip for her cats) The doll is not for domination. All this is to focus on.

*Is the spirit someone you know? Do you have something of theirs?

*You can also use runes or create a sigil to represent them.

*I'm not going through what you need for each spirit. If you don't know, you shouldn't be playing with them.

7. Rub "Spirit Summoning Oil" on the representation for a few minutes, thinking of them, and then say...

I call you_____,

Please hear my call.

Come to me_____,

With not to stall.

I ask you here,

Come to my side.

Perfect love, perfect trust,

Rules I will abide!

8. Now, wait, relax, and burn more botanicals (the ones used in oil). Hold representation close to you and speak with them...what you want and what you need; at this point, you could use a black mirror or crystal ball, etc.

9. When finished, politely ask the spirit to be on their way. Close the circle, and you're done.

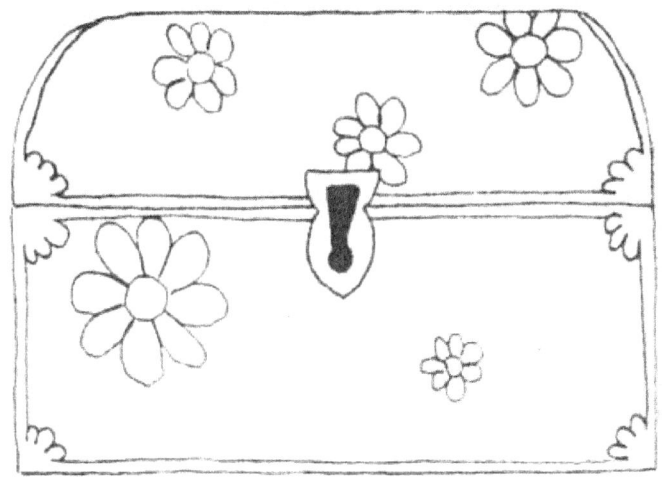

*If the spirit stays, I would wear something of iron and cast another circle. Ask the Gods for help. When you think they might be gone throw down salt at all the doors and windows.

*Make sure all items specific to this rite are put away together in an iron box.

*You could also create a seal in the middle of the floor to contain them or protect you.

Havamal-Stanza-157

"I know a twelfth one if I see, Up in a tree,

A dangling corpse in a noose;

I can carve and color the runes

That the man walks and talks with me!"

The runes to chant for this spell are...

UNWANTED SPIRIT REMOVAL

*This must be done over a 7-day period ending on the dark moon. Have someone either doing the same thing, or sending you, their energy.

*Open circle, Call Fairies, Call the Grey Wanderer, Call the Quarters, Invoke the Quarters.

"I light here a flame of warmth, joy, and life. Be with me here, Odin, Freyja, Thor, and Tyr!"

1. Light the candle you've chosen for this site.

"Oh, Great ones, I dedicate this area in your honor,

And for the magiks you create.

Be with me, in me, and of me.

Odin, the one eye,

Freyja, the beautiful,

Thor the Mighty,

Tyr the just!"

*Shake rattle, ring bell, 3 times

"I draw your spirit,

I draw you here.

Come to me, spirit; there's nothing to fear.

Leave _____ side

Bother them no more.

Tell me your problems and why you are torn,

Unwanted spirit, I bring you to me,

Come to me spirit, so mote it be!"

2. Using a grey/silver cord, tie a knot at each end representing the spell or attachment that sent the spirit in the first place.

"From sender to _____ this spell I break,

This was not right for you to make.

Its path I will abruptly end,

And back to sender the spell I send!"

> *Using a piece of paper write the name of spirit on it in runes or symbols needed. Set on fire using source candle and drop cauldron.

3. Burn or cut the cord, visualizing the spell breaking

"I release you, spirit, from this bind.

Leave this place, go to your kind.

Back to the sender, I do send,

Return to them, and let us mend!"

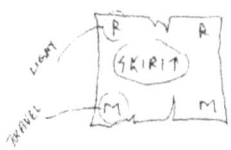

4. *Using a piece of paper, write the name of the spirit on it in runes or symbols needed. Set on fire using a source candle and drop cauldron.

118

5. Call the Gods...

"Oh great, wind-swept wanderer.

Commander of the Shining Ones.

Giver of the runes,

Chief of the wild hunt.

I call you to collect this unwanted spirit on your raid tonight.

Hail Odin! Hail Odin!"

"Oh, Queen of the Valkyries.

The one who weaves fates.

Creator of destines,

And chooser of the slain.

I call you, command your Wind Riders to take this spirit.

Hail Freyja! Hail Freyja!"

Oh, Red bearded Thunderer.

Protector of our people.

Not even the Gods can stand,

Before mighty Mjollnir.

I call to you; give me your strength.

Hail Thor! Hail Thor!"

"Oh, true, and just one.

The hand of justice.

The one who charges oaths,

And demands they're true.

I call to you; give me justice by your hand.

Hail Tyr! Hail Tyr!"

6. Add wax from the candle to the cauldron.

7. Add any herbs you use for the Gods.

8. Shake the rattle, and ring bell, 3 times

*Close circle

9. All the contents of the cauldron must be buried in the ground outside.

Note: This is never something to take on lightly. The spirit will come, and it will cause problems. If you're ready and willing, draw the spirit to yourself. Be very cautious while you're doing it. One spirit tried to split up a relationship of mine as a last resort.

*If you're really worried about your friend, draw the spirit to you for the entire 7 days. Try to get the person you're helping to wear something made of iron. This spell is totally dangerous! Make sure your friend wants the spirit gone.

*Helgrind-the gate between the living and the dead. "Death Gate"

*Garm-Monster dog who guards the underworld.

*Sleipnir (Slape-near) Odin's 8-legged horse.

Havamal-Stanza-155

"I know a tenth one if I see demons

Playing up in the air;

I can bring it about that they can't make their way back

To their own shapes,

To their own spirits!

The runes to chant for this spell are

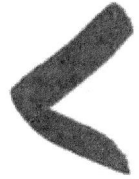

ADDICTION BANISHING

"Banishing Oil": Take the following herbs, crush them, and add them to mineral oil...Chicory-black pepper-cayenne powder-cinnamon-sea salt- powdered hydrangea-bay laurel leaves-rowan-Dragon's blood- angelica-basil

"Mojo Bag": Add a dried, crushed version of the same herbs you used for the oil. Then, add one or all of these crystals...

Amethyst-moon stone-kunzite-quart

Throw in a snakeskin for new beginnings to help shed the old you. Then a drop of your own   , and a copy of the "Strength" card when you're finished with the rite.

*All of the herbs must be found for this to have a chance!

*I like to take out my bag whenever I need it and rub it in my hands.

*Cast circle, Call Fairies, Call the Grey Wanderer, Call the Quarters, Invoke the Quarters...all on a dark moon.

1. Place all the things you'll need on your altar

2. Charge a white/purple candle with your desires

3. As you do this, carve in it the runes you'll need to help you get rid of your addiction. Also, write on it the name of your addiction

4. Rub "Banishing Oil" on the candle110

5. Place the candle in a cauldron, and place the cauldron on top of your copy of the "Devil" card covered by the "Strength" card.

*On the back of the "Devil" card, already have written the name of your addiction in runes enclosed in a circle. Likewise, on the back of the "Strength" card, have written your name and any runes that might help you in your case. Make sure the "Strength" card is on top of the "Devil" card under the cauldron.

6. Light the candle, wishing your candle will burn away your addiction, say...

"Odin, Allfather,

Give me your wisdom.

Help your kin through this horrible time.

I need to be rid of

Hail Odin! Hail Odin!"

"Freyja, Vana Goddess,

Give me your love.

Help your kin through this horrible time.

I need to be rid of

Hail Freyja! Hail Freyja!"

"Thor, Great Protector,

Give me your strength.

Help your kin through this horrible time.

I need to be rid of

Hail Thor! Hail Thor!"

7. Hold arms to the sky, say...

"My Gods, my ancestors, my people,

Hear me now.

Help me be strong and wise.

Show me your love.

Help me beat this damaging addiction of

_____

Help me be a better person.

So, I may honor you always

Hail! Hail! Hail!"

8. Take a clear bottle and imagine it's a prison for your addiction. Meditate on that for a moment.

9. Place the "Devil" card inside the bottle.

10. Put "Banishing Oil" into the bottle with the card and seal the top.

11. Tie the bottle to the bottom of 3 balloons (filled with helium) big enough to carry it away.

12. Take the "Strength" card and place it inside your "Mojo Bag".

13. Leave everything on the altar until the candle burns out on its own.

14. While it's still night, go outside with the balloons, "Banishing Oil," and burnt-out candles.

15. Take candle remains off your property and bury it in Gaia, then pour "Banishing Oil" on top of it and cover it with dirt, say...

"Be gone!"

16. Rub some "Banishing Oil" on the balloons and then hold them up in the air and say..."

So, I may be a better person!"

17. Release the balloons into the air.

*Keep your "Mojo Bag" in your pocket for as long as you need it. Rub it as much as you have to. You may have to repeat this if the addiction is really bad.

*Remember...like the meaning of the "Strength" card, you must take on this foe with your own 2 hands. Addictions don't beat themselves. I struggled for years. When you think you are alright place the "Mojo Bag" somewhere safe, you may need it again.

*Start with something small and work your way up. Don't just go big at the start and expect results.

*Finally, you must really want to get rid of this problem. Lying to yourself won't help you.

*You could also try using the "Tower" card and the "Star" card, depending on what you're doing and how deep the habit really is.

Havamal-Stanza-146

"I know those spells which the ruler's wife doesn't

know,

Nor any man's son; 'Help' one is called,

And that will help you

Against accusations and sorrows

And every sort of anxiety!

The runes to chant for this spell are...

HEX

*Warning: This is more for a reference page. Everyone in the craft should know what a hex can look like. It's the only real way to defend oneself. Only use this as a last resort. Be prepared for the backlash. In some HEX traditions, Hexing is forbidden.

*For this, we will be calling on Hella, Goddess of the Dead. Place willow, bones (any), obsidian stone, and graveyard dirt all on the altar.

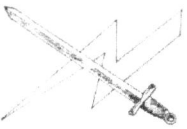

"Hex Oil": Crush, grind the following materials and add them to mineral oil...

Black pepper seeds-black mustard seeds-cayenne pepper-charcoal dust-grave yard dirt

*Open circle, Call Fairies, Call the Grey Wanderer, Call Quarters, Invoke Quarters.

1. Hold a black candle in your hands and charge it with your intentions.

2. Carve the name, preferably in full, of the target on it

3. Carve Troll Runes used for this form of spell

4. Rub your "Hex Oil" all over it well

5. Set candle in cauldron (after cleaning cauldron well)

6. Light the candle115

7. Take a picture of a target or paper with their name, and throw all your hate into it.

8. Now set it on fire using a candle, say...

"Queen of the Dead,

You who gather souls.

Hella, hear my call.

Grant me my revenge.

So that my enemies may taste true defeat.

Hail Hella! Hail Hella!"

9. Take anything you've collected of the target... Hair-nail clippings-clothing, etc.

10. Set them all on fire and add them to the cauldron contents

11. Let the candle burn out on its own.

*This is why I cut most candles in half.

12. Hold the cauldron up to the sky, say...

"Hella, Goddess of the dark,

Grant me my wish.

Let karma have its way with

Let them learn the lessons.

Hail Hella! Hail, Hella!"

*Close the circle carefully!

13. Wrap the contents of a cauldron in a black cloth

14. Now, bury it in the target yard, somewhere you know they'll pass over

15. Keep a small part of the wax clump and stab it with 3 needles. Put it on their doorstep or somewhere you know they'll touch it or pick it up.

*You can also go to their home and write the Troll Runes right on their door with "Hex Oil."

*Extra: Hella is the Goddess of the Dead and rules over Hel and Niflheim. Thus, the reason for the graveyard dirt. This Hel is not the Christian hell but a place to which most go to await rebirth. Though some wander there, confused forever

*Never forget the rules... "If it harms none, do what ye will!" and "What you send comes back!" It all comes back, whether in this lifetime or the next.

*Never bind anyone or anything in a way you would not want to be bound yourself.

Havamal-Stanza-148

"I know a third one which is very useful to me,

Which fetters my enemy;

The edges of my foes I can blunt,

Neither nor club will bite for them!"

The runes to chant for this spell are...

HEX DEFENDER

Iron Ring Spell": Take an iron ring and cleanse it fully. Wash it in rose water, then put it out for the night in direct light from a full moon. Tie it to a black ribbon, and it's ready for use.

*Iron repels ghosts and spirits well

"Hex Smashing Oil" Crush, grind the following herbs and add to mineral oil...Rose extract-cinnamon(pinch)-Dragon's blood (pinch)-sea salt (pinch) -red brick dust (pinch)

Have you been hexed? Have things gone horribly wrong? Maybe you found strange dust on your doorstep or chicken or cow parts (old-school Voodoo). Maybe it was the remains of a black candle?! If so...gather everything up, but do not bring it inside. Listen carefully...

Before you do anything, spread red brick dust and salt at your front door and any entrances.

IF YOU HAVE THE SPECIFIC ITEMS...

1. Go outside with altar items and go to an open fire pit.

2. Set up an altar with an "Iron Ring" on it.

*Cast a circle, Call Fairies, Call the Grey Wanderer, Call the Quarters, Invoke the Quarters, and start a fire pit.

3. Put on ring

4. Take items and clean them with sage/Dragon's blood and the "Hex Smashing Oil"

5. Hold a bag of gathered items up to the sky, say...

"Odin, Great Horned One, Hear my call.

Take this evil energy far away from me.

Cast it all the way down to the deep, Dark dwarves in their black calves.

Erase the hold it has on me forever more.

This I ask Shining One.

Hail Odin! Hail Odin!"

"Freyja, Beautiful Mother,

Hear my call.

Take this evil energy far away from me.

Command your Valkries to shield me

From its effects.

This I ask Earth Goddess.

Hail Freyja! Hail Freyja!"

"Thor, Bearded Thunderer,

Hear my call.

Take this evil energy far away from me.

Give me the strength of giants,

So, I might repel it myself.

This, I ask my protector.

Hail Thor! Hail Thor!"

6. Take items and cast them into the fire, say...

"I cast you back from where you came,

You know the way, you know the name

So, mote it be!"

*Close the circle and take a different way home than you came.

IF YOU DON'T HAVE THE NEEDED ITEMS...

1. Smudge with sage or Dragon's blood

2. Using the "Hex Smashing Oil," take a shower.

3. Cleanse 3 times

4. Do not use soap until the next time you shower

5. Repeat if you must

*Wear an Iron Ring for 9 days. If when you take it off, the problem is still there. It could be an unwanted spirit; you know what to do

Havamal-Stanza-149

"I know a forth one if men put

Chains upon my limbs;

I can chant so that I can walk away,

Fetters spring from my feet,

And bonds from my hands!"

The runes to chant for this spell are...

Havamal-Stanza-151

"I know a sixth one if a man wounds me

With the roots of the sap-filled wood;

That man who conjured to harm me,

The evil consumes him, not me!"

The runes to chant for this spell are...

RAGNAROK

(THE SEERESS' PROPHECY)

Baldr, "the bold and bright" son of Odin, falls to the twig of mistletoe, small and light, thrown by his blinded brother Hod, guided by Loki's hand. Baldr's brother, Vali, is born quite quickly; in his first night of life, he takes to the fight, wrapped in fetters of his own ties to life.

Loki is captured and brought to justice in a mountain cave. Sigyn, Loki's true wife, comes to his aid, and seeing him tied and chained, she must leave him in distress and takes up a bowl to collect the venom that drips from the serpents above. Whenever she leaves to empty the bowl, the venom drips upon Loki, causing the earth to shake.

The Seeress stands before all creation and looks upon the world...

To the East, poison valleys and a river of knives and swords called "Cutting." To the North stands a hall of gold in the dark-of-moon plains and the giant's beer hall on the never-cooled plain. To the West, a hall made of serpent's spines, dripping with venom and with doors facing the North, Corpse- strand stands is its name. Then she saw fallen men drowning in steams of agony. Those who swear false oaths and bespeak treachery. Wolves tear at flesh, and Nidhogg sucks the bones of the dead clean.

An old giantess, Iarnsaxa, in Iron-wood, nurtures the two offspring of Fenrir. Doomed men fall, and the halls of the Gods flow with crimson blood. The day becomes night, and the storms are vicious. A bright-red Rooster calls in Gallows-wood as Eggther, the giantess' herdsman, plucks his harp.

Fjalar wakens the Aesir, warriors at the Father of Hosts. A dark sooty-red cock bellows in the halls of the Underworld. Garm, the raven, will run free as his fetters break, and he howls loudly as a warning to all who can hear it.

Brother slays brother, bonds of kinship are broken, and no man will spare another. Gjallar-horn is sounded, Heimdall blows loudly, and Odin converses with Mimir's head.

Yggdrasill shudders and groans through all the chaos, and the ship of the dead breaks lose its ties. Loki, having broken free, travels with his monstrous brood from Muspell's shores to do battle to the end. The rocky cliffs crack open, and Hella comes forth as the skies split apart and men walk the road of Hel.

Odin advances to his doom in his fight against the Fenrir wolf, as it's been foretold, and falls honorably as Frigga weeps. Vidar, Odin's son, slays the beast with a stab of his sword to its heart, avenging his father. All the Gods match up against their chosen foes, and the great battle truly begins.

Gapping in the air, the jaws of the World Serpent part. Thor takes up his mighty weapon, Mjollnir, and strikes down the massive reptile, killing the beast. Afterward, he takes but nine steps and falls victim to its venom.

Middle Earth sinks into the sea, and the stars wink out from the sky. After three years, the earth rises from the sea once more, green and renewed, and the animals are restored. Fields grow without being sowed, and all aliments will be banished.

A man, Lifthrasir, and a woman, Lif, have been protected all this time to renew the human race. Now, they come forth to take on their task, as Baldr is reborn to take up his father's place on the throne of the Aesir in the hall named Gimli.

GLOSSERY

Aesir: one of the 2 races of Gods.

Asatru: the Norse religion, best known for the Vikings, means "True to the Aesir" and has ties as far back as 1000-2000 BC.

Asgard: home to the race of Gods, the Aesir.

Astral Travel: a person's spirit leaving the body on a journey

Arvind: Odin, as the giant that brings the runes to their race, also means "friend".

Baldr: son of Odin, his death brings about the Ragnarok.

Banishing: getting rid of something physically, mentally, and spiritually.

Bind or Binding: to bring two people, animals, or things together as one.

Bind rune: two or more runes superimposed on top of each other to create another.

Black Mirror: a reflective surface, usually a piece of glass painted black on the back, created to commune with spirits or see the future.

Brisingamen: Freyja's magical necklace.

Casting: creating a magical space for doing rituals or spellcraft. Cauldron: a giant pot, usually made of iron, used as a representation of the Goddess' womb of rebirth.

Charging: putting all your will and intentions into something. Dain: Odin as the elf that brings the runes to their race. Dark moon: the opposite of a full moon, when the moon is done Waxing and just before it begins to wane.

Dvalin: Odin is the Dwarf that brings the runes to their race.

Edda refers to the titles of ancient manuscripts, sagas, and myth stories.

Eggther: the giantess Iarnsaxa's shepherd.

Fairies: also known as the "other people," they are usually the size of sprites or pixies but can be bigger.

Familiar: usually an animal that a person has a strong psychic bond with.

Fenrir: offspring of Loki, a giant monstrous wolf that consumes Odin in Ragnarok125

Fetch: an external aspect of the self that appears in the form of a spirit beast of power.

Freyja: Vana-Goddess (Vanir), mistress to Odin, Goddess of love and lust, means "Lady."

Frigga: Odin's Wife or consort, Keeper of the golden apples that keep the Gods young, and weaver of the string used by the Norns to control man's fate.

Futhark: the oldest set of runes, created before 400 CE, also called the "Elder" or "Germanic." Futhark derives its name from the first 6 runes' phonetical value when put in its original order.

Garm: the monstrous dog that guards the underworld. Gimli: the last Aesir Hall standing after Ragnarok.

Godi: a priest.

Godia: a priestess.

Hamingja: usually described as luck or karma passed down from one lifetime to another.

Hand-Fastening: a marriage or binding of two people.

Havamal: sayings of the High One (Odin), translations of his words. Heimdal blows the horn of Gjallar and wakes the Gods to Ragnarok.

Hel: ruled by the Goddess Hella, where the dead live until rebirth.

Hella: Goddess of the underworld.

Hex: someone wishing ill will on you, bad luck or karma, a curse.

Hod: the blind brother of Baldr who throws the twig of mistletoe and kills him.

Iarnsaxa: the old giantess that lives in Ironwood and nurtures the two offspring of Fenrir.

Invoke: to draw in the power and energy of something, to become one with some energy force.

Jotunheim: home to the frost-giants, a world of chaos.

Lif: the first woman after Ragnarok.

Lifthrasir: the first man after Ragnarok.

Lightalfheim: home to the Light Elves, or Elves.

Loki: trickster of the Pantheon, shapeshifter, father of Fenrir. Magi: Warriors in the desert of ancient times.

Magik: I prefer to write magic this way. The utilizing and manipulating of cosmic forces to do one's bidding.

Middle Earth: see Midgard.

Midgard: what the Norse called Earth.

Mimir: the guardian of the well of knowledge.

Mjollnir: Thor's mighty hammer.

Mojo: the essence of someone, karma, virility, energy.

Muspelheim: also called Muspell, it's the world of creative and destructive fire.

Nidhogg: the dragon that gnaws at the roots of Yggdrasill.

Nifelheim: controlled by the dragon Nidhogg, it's a world of creative and destructive cold.

Norns: like the three "fates" of the Greek tradition. They are female representations of past, present, and future.

Odin: Chief God of the Aesir, the Hooded One, Allfather, the Grey Wanderer, Chief of the Wild Hunt, Collector of half the slain, wizard and warrior.

Ogam: language used by the Celtic peoples depicted with lines that are vertical, horizontal, and diagonal.

Psychopomps: messengers of the dead.

Quarters: the four directions on a compass, North, East, South, West.

Ragnarok: the apocalypse, the end of the world, the new beginning, the Doom of the Gods.

Rede: statement of intent or purpose.

Rite: a ritual

Runes: ancient script used for magical writing and telling the myths from generation to generation, created before 400 CE., usually represented by the Germanic Futhark.

Runic Divination: telling the future by using the runes.

Samhain: for some pagans, it's the beginning of the year, closely associated with Halloween and the Celts, also called "Night of the Spectres."

Seals: a ward used to protect someone, somewhere, or something, symbols of control.

Seeress: the seeress' prophecy (Voluspa), like the Oracle of Greece, remembers the beginning of the world and can see past Ragnarok.

Seidr: a type of Spellcraft usually done by women.

Sigil: a symbol created by the Witches' Wheel.

Sigyn: Loki's wife.

Spellcraft: the use of magical knowledge to change one's own surroundings or fate to throw magic.

Stanzas: paragraphs in the Eddas. Summon: to draw to you.

Swartalfheim means "home of the dark elves"; it's the world of the dwarves.

Talisman: a piece of jewelry worn for protection against someone or something, usually created by hand specifically for this purpose.

Tarot Cards: cards used to tell the future.

Theban: an ancient alphabet now adopted by Wiccans, also called the "Witches' alphabet."

Thor: Odin's son, the red-bearded thunderer, protector of men; his mother was a giant.

Troll Runes: a bastardized version of the runes used for curses and hexes.

Tyr: the God of justice and oaths.

Underworld: Usually depicted as Hel (not the Christian hell), one of the nine worlds of the Asatru religion.

Vadar: Baldr's brother and son of Odin.

Valhalla (Valhall): Hall of heroes, one of the halls Odin resides in, where all the fallen warriors wait until Ragnarok.

Valkyries: shield maidens, collectors of the slain, and protectors of men in battle, usually numbering 9 to 13.Vanaheim: home to the race of Gods, the Vanir.

Vanir: the second race of Gods.

Waning: when the moon is beginning to be uncovered by the earth's shadow.

Waxing: when the moon is beginning to be covered by the earth's shadow.

Witches' Pyramid: a drawn representation of some of the lessons learned by WitchesWitches'

Wheel: a wheel of letters used to create symbols for magikal work.

World Serpent: Earth-girdle, a giant serpent in the sea and Thor's nemesis.

Wyrd: the enter-locking strands of fate that tie us all together. Yggdrasill: the tree of life, rooted in all 9 worlds of the Norse religion

NOTES

Chapter 1: The Laws of Old

Rede of Honour

- ☐ Ed Fitch. Rites of Odin. Llewellyn Publications. 1990, 2003

Chapter 2: Casting Your Circle

Calling of the Grey Wanderer

- ☐ Ed Fitch. Rites of Odin. Llewellyn Publications. 1990, 2003

Calling Quarters

- ☐ Carolyne Larrington. The Poetic Edda, a New Translation. Oxford University Press. 1996.

Invoking the Power of the 4 Quarters

- ☐ D. J. Conway. Norse Magic. Llewellyn World Magic Series. Llewellyn Publications. 2003

Chapter 3: Spellcraft Basics

Charge of the Goddess

- ☐ Doreen Valiente The Nine Worlds Freya Aswynn. Northern Mysteries and Magic, Runes and Feminine Powers. Llewellyn Publications. 1990, 2002

Witches' Wheel

- ☐ Ann Moura. Green Witchcraft III, the Manual. Llewellyn Publications. 2000, 2002

Black Mirror

- Ann Moura. Green Witchcraft II, Balancing Light, and Dark. Llewellyn Publications. 1999, 2003

Chapter 4: The Viking Oracle

Runes

- Freya Aswynn. Northern Mysteries and Magic, Runes and Feminine Powers. Llewellyn Publications. 1990, 2002
- Paul Rhys Mountfort. Nordic Runes, Understanding, Casting, and Interpreting the Ancient Viking Oracle. Destiny Books. 2003
- Edred Thorson. Runelore, A Handbook of Esoteric Runeology. Red Wheel/Wieser, Llc. 1987
- Jennifer Smith. Raido, the Runic Journey. (self-published) P.O.Box 23074, 55 Ontario St. Milton, Ontario, Canada L9T 5B4. 1993, 1994

Runic Divination

- Freya Aswynn. Northern Mysteries and Magic, Runes and Feminine Powers. Llewellyn Publications. 1990, 2002
- Paul Rhys Mountfort. Nordic Runes, Understanding, Casting, and Interpreting the Ancient Viking Oracle. Destiny Books. 2003
- Edred Thorson. Runelore, A Handbook of Esoteric Runeology. Red Wheel/Wieser, Llc. 1987
- Jennifer Smith. Raido, the Runic Journey. (self-published) P.O.Box 23074, 55 Ontario St. Milton, Ontario, Canada L9T 5B4. 1993, 1994.

Troll Runesto

Bernard King. Runes, an introductory Guide Interpreting the Ancient Wisdom of the Runes. Element Books. 2003

Chapter 5: Potions

Dream Potion: Delfino's Mugwort Tea

- ☐ Judika Illes. Elemental Encyclopaedia of 5000 Spells is the ultimate reference book for the magical arts. HarperCollins Publishers, Ltd. Harper element. 2004

Beautiful Mead

- ☐ Ed Fitch. Rites of Odin. Llewellyn Publications. 1990, 2003.
- ☐ D.J.Conway. Norse Magic. Llewellyn World Magic Series. Llewellyn Publications. 2003

Chapter 6: Animal Allies

A Cat's History

- ☐ National Geographic Channel. The National Geographic Society. (Documentary). "The Science of Cats"

Familiar Connection

- ☐ Judika Illes. Elemental Encyclopaedia of 5000 Spells is the ultimate reference book for the magical arts. HarperCollins Publishers, Ltd. Harper element. 2004
- ☐ Carolyne Larrington. The Poetic Edda, a New Translation. Oxford University Press. 1996.Initiation•2003

Chapter 7: Rites & Ritual

Initiation

- Ed Fitch. Rites of Odin. Llewellyn Publications. 1990, 2003
- Ann Moura. Green Witchcraft, Folk Magic, Fairy Lore and Herb Craft. Llewellyn Publications. 1999, 2003
- D.J.Conway. Norse Magic. Llewellyn World Magic Series. Llewellyn Publications. 2003
- Carolyne Larrington. The Poetic Edda, a New Translation. Oxford University Press. 1996.

Hand Fastening

- Ed Fitch. Rites of Odin. Llewellyn Publications. 1990, 2003.

Shamanic Transformation

- Freya Aswynn. Northern Mysteries and Magic, Runes and Feminine Powers. Llewellyn Publications. 1990, 2002
- Carolyne Larrington. The Poetic Edda, a New Translation. Oxford University Press. 1996.
- Judika Illes. Elemental Encyclopaedia of 5000 Spells, the ultimate reference book for the magical arts. HarperCollins Publishers, Ltd. Harper element. 2004

Astral Travel

- Judika Illes. Elemental Encyclopaedia of 5000 Spells, the ultimate reference book for the magical arts. HarperCollins Publishers, Ltd. Harper element. 2004
- Carolyne Larrington. The Poetic Edda, a New Translation. Oxford University Press. 1996.

Baby Maker

- Judika Illes. Elemental Encyclopaedia of 5000 Spells, the ultimate reference book for the magical arts. HarperCollins Publishers, Ltd. Harper element. 2004
- Carolyne Larrington. The Poetic Edda, a New Translation. Oxford University Press. 1996.

Chapter 8: Spells & Incantations

Love Maker

- Judika Illes. Elemental Encyclopaedia of 5000 Spells, the ultimate reference book for the magical arts. HarperCollins Publishers, Ltd. Harper element. 2004
- Ann Moura. Green Witchcraft, Folk Magic, Fairy Lore and Herb Craft. Llewellyn Publications.-1999, 2003
- D.J.Conway. Norse Magic. Llewellyn World Magic Series. Llewellyn Publications. 2003
- Carolyne Larrington. The Poetic Edda, a New Translation. Oxford University Press. 1996.

Healing Spell

- Judika Illes. Elemental Encyclopaedia of 5000 Spells, the ultimate reference book for the magical arts. HarperCollins Publishers, Ltd. Harper element. 2004
- Ed Fitch. Rites of Odin. Llewellyn Publications. 1990,2003
- Carolyne Larrington. The Poetic Edda, a New Translation. Oxford University Press. 1996.

Call for Justice

- Judika Illes. Elemental Encyclopaedia of 5000 Spells, the ultimate reference book for the magical arts. HarperCollins Publishers, Ltd. Harper element. 2004

☐ Ed Fitch. Rites of Odin. Llewellyn Publications. 1990, 2003

☐ Carolyne Larrington. The Poetic Edda, a New Translation. Oxford University Press. 1996.

☐ Carolyne Larrington. The Poetic Edda, a New Translation. Oxford University Press. 1996.

Spell of Persuasion

☐ Judika Illes. Elemental Encyclopaedia of 5000 Spells, the ultimate reference book for the magical arts. HarperCollins Publishers, Ltd. Harper element. 2004

☐ Carolyne Larrington. The Poetic Edda, a New Translation. Oxford University Press. 1996

Death & Dying

☐ Judika Illes. Elemental En cyclopaedia of 5000 Spells, the ultimate reference book for the magical arts. HarperCollins Publishers, Ltd. Harper element. 2004

☐ Carolyne Larrington. The Poetic Edda, a New Translation. Oxford University Press. 1996.

☐ Carolyne Larrington. The Poetic Edda, a New Translation. Oxford University Press. 1996.

Spirit Summons

☐ Judika Illes. Elemental Encyclopaedia of 5000 Spells, the ultimate reference book for the magical arts. HarperCollins Publishers, Ltd. Harper element. 2004

☐ Carolyne Larrington. The Poetic Edda, a New Translation. Oxford University Press. 1996.

☐ Carolyne Larrington. The Poetic Edda, a New Translation. Oxford University Press. 1996.

Unwanted Spirit Removal

- Ed Fitch. Rites of Odin. Llewellyn Publications. 1990, 2003
- D.J.Conway. Norse Magic. Llewellyn World Magic Series. Llewellyn Publications. 2003
- Carolyne Larrington. The Poetic Edda, a New Translation. Oxford University Press. 1996.

Addiction Banishing

- Judika Illes. Elemental Encyclopaedia of 5000 Spells, the ultimate reference book for the magical arts. HarperCollins Publishers, Ltd. Harper element. 2004
- Ed Fitch. Rites of Odin. Llewellyn Publications. 1990, 2003.
- Carolyne Larrington. The Poetic Edda, a New Translation. Oxford University Press. 1996.

Hex

- Judika Illes. Elemental Encyclopaedia of 5000 Spells, the ultimate reference book for the magical arts. HarperCollins Publishers, Ltd. Harper element. 2004
- D.J.Conway. Norse Magic. Llewellyn World Magic Series. Llewellyn Publications. 2003
- Carolyne Larrington. The Poetic Edda, a New Translation. Oxford University Press. 1996.

Hex Defender

- Judika Illes. Elemental Encyclopaedia of 5000 Spells, the ultimate reference book for the magical arts. HarperCollins Publishers, Ltd. Harper element. 2004
- Ed Fitch. Rites of Odin. Llewellyn Publications. 1990, 2003.

- Carolyne Larrington. The Poetic Edda, a New Translation. Oxford University Press. 1996.

Ragnarok

- Carolyne Larrington. The Poetic Edda, a New Translation. Oxford University Press. 1996.
- H.A.Guerber. Myths of the Norsemen, from the Eddas and Sagas. Dover Publication, Inc. New York. 1992.

BIBLIOGRAPHY

1. Judika Illes. Elemental Encyclopaedia of 5000 Spells, the ultimate reference book for the magical arts. HarperCollins Publishers, Ltd. Harper element. 2004

2. Ed Fitch. Rites of Odin. Llewellyn Publications. 1990, 2003

3. D.J. Conway. Norse Magic. Llewellyn World Magic Series. Llewellyn Publications. 2003

4. Ann Moura. Green Witchcraft, Folk Magic, Fairy Lore and Herb Craft. Llewellyn Publications. 1999, 2003

5. Ann Moura. Green Witchcraft II, Balancing Light and Dark. Llewellyn Publications. 1999, 2003

6. Ann Moura. Green Witchcraft III, the Manual. Llewellyn Publications. 2000, 2002

7. Freya Aswynn. Northern Mysteries and Magic, Runes and Feminine Powers. Llewellyn Publications. 1990, 2002to

8. Bernard King. Runes, an introductory Guide Interpreting the Ancient Wisdom of the Runes. Element Books. 2003

9. Paul Rhys Mountfort. Nordic Runes, Understanding, Casting, and Interpreting the Ancient Viking Oracle. Destiny Books. 2003

10. Edred Thorson. Runelore, A Handbook of Esoteric Runeology. Red Wheel/Wieser, Llc. 1987(self

11. Jennifer Smith. Raido, the Runic Journey. published) P.O.Box 23074, 55 Ontario St. Milton, Ontario, Canada, L9T 5B4. 1993, 1994.

12. Carolyne Larrington. The Poetic Edda, a New Translation. Oxford University Press. 1996.

13. "The Brewers Guild of the Asatru Free Assembly"

14. Arthur Edward Waite. Rider-Waite Tarot Deck. Rider Company of London. 1910.

15. H.A.Guerber. Myths of the Norsemen, from the Eddas and Sagas. Dover Publication, Inc. New York. 1992.

16. The National Geographic Channel, The National Geographic Society. "The Science of Cats" Documentary

START DOWN YOUR PATH

TOWARDS NORSE

SPELLCRAFT!

HERE IN THESE PAGES IS EVERYTHING YOU NEED TO KNOW TO START THE LONG ROAD OF SPELLCRAFT. FROM MY OWN "BOOK OF SHADOWS" I'VE INCLUDED...

- Herbs

- Incense

- Oils

- Runes, and how to carve them

- Pictures of tarot cards for reference

- Gods and Goddesses

- Chants

- Invocations

- Rituals

- Spells

- And how to create anything else you might need to do this work

As a second-generation witch I feel it's my honor to spread the word and writings of our people across the land. I believe it's time that the world remembers its beginnings and where it came from. I feel a new beginning is close at hand for our pagan and heathen brothers and sisters. Always remember that when we strengthen our people, they strengthen us in return.

"In perfect love and perfect trust, we prevail!"

"Hail Odin!"

www.ingramcontent.com/pod-product-compliance
Lightning Source LLC
Chambersburg PA
CBHW041627140626
46547CB00031B/1153